M000204393

Also in the Star Book for Ministers series

Available now:
The Star Book for Ministers
Edward T. Hiscox

The Star Book for Ministers Gift Edition
Edward T. Hiscox

The Star Book on Preaching
Marvin A. McMickle

The Star Book for Stewardship
Clifford A. Jones Sr.

The Star Book for Pastoral Counseling
Jason Richard Curry

www.judsonpress.com / 800-4-JUDSON

The
STAR BOOK
for
PASTORAL COUNSELING

Jason Richard Curry

JUDSON PRESS
PUBLISHERS SINCE 1824

Join our mailing list for updates and special offers.

www.judsonpress.com/mailing_list.cfm

Library of Congress Cataloging-in-Publication Data
Curry, Jason Richard. The star book for pastoral counseling
/Jason Richard Curry.—First Edition, 2013.
pages cm
ISBN 978-0-8170-1685-2 (hardcover: alk. paper) 1. Pastoral
counseling. I. Title.
BV4012.2.C87 2013
253.5—dc23

2012034277

Printed in the U.S.A.
First Edition, 2013.

Preface

The theory and the practice of pastoral care and counseling presented in this handbook are necessarily informed by my experiences in clinical, academic, and ecclesiastical arenas. The content of the handbook is informed by some of my experiences as a youth and teenage parishioner at Agape African Methodist Episcopal Church in Buffalo, New York; as youth minister at Payne Chapel African Methodist Episcopal Church in Nashville, Tennessee; as an assistant minister at Charles Street African Methodist Episcopal Church in Boston, Massachusetts; as pastor of both St. Matthew African Methodist Episcopal Church and St. Peter African Methodist Episcopal Church in Kentucky; as an inpatient and outpatient counselor at the Dimock Community Health Center in Roxbury, Massachusetts; as a PhD student in religion and personality at Vanderbilt University; and as assistant professor of religious and philosophical studies, also an assistant professor of Psychology, and dean of the chapel at Fisk University.

Over the past twenty years in these various contexts I have had the opportunity to provide counseling to African Americans, European Americans, teenagers, individuals addicted to alcohol and other drugs, individuals who embrace the Judeo-Christian concept of God, individuals who choose to ignore the attributes of God within a Judeo-Christian context and simply recognize God as a Higher Power, couples who are considering marriage and divorce, families who are coping with the stages of grief as a result of the loss of a loved one, students, faculty, and administrators within a university context and individuals in transitional care facilities (e.g., halfway houses and short-term residential rehabilitation centers). I have seen people achieve insight regarding the nature of their presenting problems, and I have seen people fail to reach the goals listed in their treatment plan.

I often see an aspect of myself in clients whom I am facing across a desk, and I recognize that, given a few more challenges in life, I may have been sitting where they were sitting. Furthermore, I perceive that if these clients or parishioners were given a few more resources and words of encouragement in their lives, they could have been sitting where I sit as a counselor.

I have made painstaking efforts to protect the identities of the people mentioned throughout this book as well as the clinical material that was expressed in confidence. At the same time, the sections of the case studies presented throughout this handbook are based upon my actual encounters with individuals, couples, and families. The techniques that proved to be successful with some individuals, couples, and families were not as effective as I would have liked them to have been with other individuals, couples, and families. Nevertheless, the lessons learned from working with these individuals proved to have intrinsic as well as extrinsic value for me, and I pray that they will have value for my readers. Ultimately, I hope that my successes in working with people who viewed me as a counselor in general and a pastoral counselor in particular will help new and seasoned clergy to address problems that are readily apparent in the behavior or buried deep within the thoughts of their parishioners.

Jason Richard Curry

Acknowledgments

A variety of pastoral figures as well as a host of experiences in the parish ministry have provided the inspiration for writing this book. The pastoral counselors who have helped me to address challenges in my intrapersonal as well as interpersonal life can be found across racial, denominational, and gender lines. In my opinion, these individuals have truly embodied Seward Hiltner's notion of the "Shepherd Motif"[1] inasmuch as they dared to reveal aspects about themselves or their ministries in an effort to further my growth and development as a person who provides pastoral care and counseling in a university community. I am indebted to the following pastors and former pastors within the African Methodist Episcopal Church for their advice and counsel over the course of four decades: Bishop Vashti McKenzie, Bishop H. H. Brookins, Bishop Fredrick Hilborn Talbot, Rev. Dr. Fred Lucas, Rev. Dr. Gregory G. Groover, and Rev. Sydney Bryant. These individuals have provided effective pastoral care and counseling to their congregations within African

Methodism for decades, and they have also made a tremendous investment in my life.

I am also indebted to the following individuals within the Baptist church for their advice, patience, and counsel for more than four decades regarding effective strategies for addressing problems that appear and exist among parishioners: Rev. Dr. Calvin Butts, Rev. Dr. Cheryl Townsend-Gilkes, Rev. Dr. Raphael Warnock, Rev. Dr. Clarence James, President Robert Michael Franklin Jr. (Morehouse College), Rev. Dr. Charles Adams, Rev. Dr. Otis Moss Jr., Rev. Dr. Otis Moss III, Rev. Dr. Clarence James, and Rev. Dr. Lawrence Edward Carter. These individuals have proven to be great listeners, and although they are great preachers of the gospel, they also have understood the classic distinction between preaching and counseling. Their understanding of the complex but complementary aspects of the Christian experience have helped countless parishioners overcome problems in their personal lives.

I would also like to express my gratitude to the administrators, faculty, and students of Fisk University for assisting me with the overall construction of this publication. In particular, I would like to thank President Hazel R. O'Leary for providing me with the time and space during the summer months to complete the manuscript, members of the faculty for their insights about the relationship between psychology and religion, and my students, especially the Chapel Assistants, for their encouragement, patience, and overall assistance during the completion of the manuscript. I am indeed thankful for the entire Fisk Family as it concerns the academic, financial, and spiritual support that was provided to me so that I could complete this project.

I am indebted to the following "icons of the academy" for helping me to formulate a theoretical and theological framework for understanding the processes and techniques associated with effective pastoral care and counseling. I thank the late Rev. Dr. Liston Mills, Dr. Bonnie-Miller McLemore, Dr. Victor Anderson, and Dr. Volney Gay of Vanderbilt University. My experiences as a doctoral student in the area of religion and personality with the Graduate Department of Religion have afforded me the opportunity to spend quality time (sometimes hours on end) with individuals who helped me to integrate my religious sensibilities with the extant psychological theories regarding the self as well as the self in community. They proved to be courageous mentors who pushed me beyond my theological and psychological comfort zones.

As mentors, they provided advice that was both solicited and unsolicited; however, their observations and criticisms were always insightful and therefore helpful. My academic papers often bled of red ink, and my initial assessment of the intrapersonal dynamics operative in the lives of some of the residents of Matthew 25 (a short-term residential facility in Nashville, Tennessee), who received pastoral counseling from me, were inaccurate; nevertheless, the intent of the pedagogy of my academic mentors was unmistakably clear: "Continue to further your understanding of the integration of the fields of psychology, theology, and culture, and formulate or improve upon a coherent and consistent method of integrating psychological theory with the insights of theology in order to provide pastoral care and counseling to individuals, couples, and families. Also, design or implement a tool to measure your success, to duplicate your success and publish the results." I am still working hard to fulfill that mandate.

Although circumstances often prohibit me from continuing to benefit from their counsel on a consistent basis, I vividly recall the profound impact that all of the aforementioned individuals have made on my pastoral counseling ministry, and I constantly look forward to the opportunity to continue to understand and help as a result of my experiences with them.

Lastly, I thank my wife, Angela, for being supportive of this project from beginning to end. In many ways, she is my pastoral counselor, and I thank God for allowing us to meet somewhere between Morehouse and Spelman. I also thank my children, John, Sam, and Nia, for a wealth of rich experiences to help families with children in need of pastoral counseling.

Notes

1. See Seward Hiltner, *Pastoral Theology: The Ministry and Theory of Shepherding* (New York: Abingdon Press, 1958), 15–20.

Introduction

It is challenging, if not impossible, to embark on this literary project regarding the theory and practice of pastoral counseling within a parish and postmodern context without mentioning its relationship to the broader category of pastoral care. Pastoral care is an individual and corporate activity that refers to a range of services and ministries that positively impact people within a parish context. Examples of ministries designed to provide pastoral care within a parish context include the bereavement ministry, the food pantry ministry, the choir, the exercise ministry, and the single adult ministry. Examples of pastoral care outside of the walls of the local church include ministry to the incarcerated, ministry to the homeless through a local shelter, and ministry to those addicted to alcohol and other drugs at a transitional care facility. Those who are offering pastoral care to others may utilize the resources of the church (e.g., money collected through tithes and offerings), as opposed to government funds, in order to help persons in need.

Pastoral care necessarily occurs with the authority and guidance of the pastor, even if he or she delegates specific responsibilities to someone else. Pastoral counseling is a specific ministry within the broader context of pastoral care. Broadly speaking, pastoral counseling refers to the art and skill associated with listening to the narratives or stories of individuals in an attempt to discover the nature of the problem that is confronting them. In order to assist them in their efforts to resolve the problem, the pastoral counselor utilizes the resources provided by the disciplines of psychology and theology. The chapters within this handbook primarily concern the techniques and insights regarding pastoral counseling that I have found to be effective over the years. Even though this handbook is written primarily for clergy, I believe that the laity, professors, students, and individuals from other disciplines can benefit from the content and techniques presented in this book.

The purpose of this book is to provide new and seasoned clergy with a concise resource for understanding the theory and practice of pastoral counseling in an ecclesiastical and postmodern context. The Bible remains the most significant and authoritative book in the lives of most Christians, and the Holy Spirit continues to enliven and unfold richer meanings in the Scriptures. At the same time, these ancient and traditional spiritual resources may be supplemented to respond to circumstances that confront us in the twenty-first century—circumstances that often present challenging new experiences not specifically or extensively addressed in the sixty-six books of the biblical canon. Therefore, resources need to be developed and implemented in a timely manner in order to address the psychological and emotional crises of the present day.

Such new resources for pastors must be created because the existential circumstances in which people find themselves often change from generation to generation. For example, the prophet Amos emphasized the theme of justice and righteousness, which helped to provide the theological basis for African American and European American clergy who were actively involved in the Civil Rights movement of the twentieth century. Those same texts may now be read against the backdrop of the blatant economic disparities that exist between countries and the citizens of those countries who have been negatively impacted by the global economy. It is clear that the environmental circumstances in which people find themselves change even if the theological truths that serve as pillars of the Christian message stay the same (e.g., the reality of God's presence and love in our lives).

Therefore, this book is an attempt to provide clergy with an additional resource to respond to new and often perplexing crises that confront the congregants of any given church. In short, this book is a resource created by a pastor for pastors who are attempting to address the multitude of interpersonal, intrapersonal, and extrapersonal challenges faced by parishioners in the twenty-first century.

The Star Book for Pastoral Counseling is primarily written for clergy who are interested in providing pastoral care and counseling to the people whom they see on a daily or weekly basis within the church. This handbook is also intended for individuals who are interested in providing pastoral care and counseling in mental health, treatment facilities (e.g., hospitals), and pastoral counseling centers. Lastly, it is intended to be a resource for students and professors who are interested in furthering their understanding of the theory and practice of pastoral care and counseling. Given that the poles on the spectrum of practical theology range from individuals who are primarily interested in understanding and interpreting religious phenomena with insights provided by the social sciences (e.g., psychologists and psychiatrists) to individuals who have a professional identity that overtly seeks to promote and embrace some aspect of religious experience (e.g., pastors who are interested in providing pastoral care and counseling to their parishioners), a diversity of professional identities necessarily exists among individuals who provide counseling to parishioners.

For example, a psychiatrist who is providing counseling to an individual who attends church may initially interpret the "voice of God" that is heard by that parishioner as clear evidence of a mental disorder (e.g., an Axis I diagnosis of schizophrenia), whereas a pastor may recognize this same "voice of God" heard by the parishioner as an experience with or revelation from God. Again, in this instance, the psychiatrist and the pastoral counselor represent opposite poles of the practical theology spectrum. It is the behavior of the parishioner who hears the "voice" that will ultimately determine if this auditory phenomenon is evidence of pathology.

Because this handbook is primarily intended for individuals who are concerned with the pastoral care and counseling end of the practical theology spectrum (i.e., clergy attempting to provide pastoral counseling to their parishioners), the presence of clinical material (e.g., voices heard by parishioners or dreams experienced by parishioners) will be discussed and interpreted throughout this handbook primarily through theological, as opposed to clinical, lenses.

The goal of the handbook is to help both clergy counselors and lay clients affirm the tenants of the Christian faith while they are confronting the variety of intrapsychic processes and theological experiences that impact parishioners. As a member of the clergy, I believe that the resources of the Christian tradition (e.g., prayer and reading the Bible) are capable of helping parishioners to address anxieties and conflicts in their daily lives. Even though I have received clinical training as a counselor at the Dimock Community Health Center in Roxbury, Massachusetts, I am writing this handbook primarily from the perspective of a minister who has (1) benefited from the practice of pastoral counseling at the Vine Street Pastoral Counseling Center in Nashville, Tennessee, from Dr. James Coffman, and (2) provided pastoral care and counseling as a senior pastor and as a dean of the chapel in a university context. Although this handbook is intended to be a resource for clinicians as well as those affiliated in some way with the academy, it is written primarily by a member of the clergy to new and seasoned clergy who are interested in providing effective pastoral care and counseling in a parish context.

The counseling process is a creative one that is necessarily informed by the data and/or insights provided by the social sciences as well as the unique personality of the pastoral counselor. Even if a group of pastoral counselors were of the same gender, were graduates of the same institutions of higher education, and were serving as clergy in parishes within the same denomination, (1) the emphasis that each pastoral counselor placed on certain scriptural passages, (2) the revelations that each pastoral counselor received from God regarding the nature of the presenting spiritual problem, and (3) the analysis of the human personality that each pastoral counselor formed that is shaped by his or her ideas on race, class, gender, and/or orientation would vary from pastoral counselor to pastoral counselor.

Given that the environmental factors that confront people are constantly changing, the counseling process must be a creative and flexible process that necessarily evolves within the parish context. Certain processes within the pastoral counseling process must be responsive to ever-changing times and people in order for the discipline of pastoral counseling to become a more comprehensive process and arena for understanding persons. Therefore, this handbook can represent only a brief overview of some of the theoretical perspectives, psychological techniques, and theological insights that I have found to be effective in helping people within a parish and university context. In other words, it is not a definitive guide detailing the art and skill associated with the pastoral care and counseling process within the parish context. Inasmuch as the Holy Spirit continues to provide revelations to women and men regarding the nature of problems that present themselves in the counseling process, this handbook is incapable of presenting an exhaustive account of God's revelatory power as expressed in the counseling process.

The postmodern era will continue to demand that people discover news truths about their ever-changing social location. This book is an introduction to the theory and practice of pastoral care and counseling within a postmodern and ecclesiastical context. It is intended to inspire new and seasoned clergy to become lifelong learners in the pastoral counseling process. It is also meant to be used as a brief guide for helping the individuals, couples, and families of the church who are experiencing crises in their personal, professional, and spiritual lives. Lastly, this handbook is intended to provide hope to pastoral counselors who have a sincere desire to help persons in need, even if these counselors are pastors who do not have the time or opportunity to review the theories associated with the counseling process. This handbook represents a brief but significant part of the entire pastoral counseling process, and I pray that it will be a resource for clergy as well as other caregivers seeking to help God's people.

Pastoral Counseling: The Basics

1. The Meaning of Pastoral Care

The term *pastoral care* refers to the broad range of ministries and services provided by a local church or denominational body that seek to ameliorate suffering and angst among people by providing them with hope and healing within or outside of the walls of a church. The theological point of departure for the idea and practice of pastoral care is firmly rooted in the second of the two great commandments as stated by Jesus: "'Love the Lord your God with all your heart, and with all your soul, and with all your mind.' This is first and greatest commandment. And a second is like it: 'Love your neighbor as yourself.' All the Law and the Prophets hang on these two commandments." (Matthew 22:37-40). The Scriptures also remind us that we serve a God who is omniscient (all-knowing [1 John 3:20]), omnipresent (everywhere [Psalm 139:7-10]), and omnipotent (all-powerful [Matthew 19:26]).

It is also important to note that we serve a God who is transcendent (exalted above us) as well as immanent (close by us) in nature. The immanent nature or attribute of God is captured in the person and presence of Jesus the Christ.

Pastoral care represents the church's individual and corporate response to caring for people in a manner in which the immanent God, Jesus the Christ, demonstrated care and concern for the blind, the diseased, and the sick people of his day. As followers of Christ and leaders of God's people within a parish context, Christian leaders have both a biblical mandate and moral obligation to exemplify the attributes of divinity wrapped in humanity through the care and concern of those within their congregation. Consider John 4:1-26, in which Jesus, who was of Jewish descent, demonstrated care and concern for a woman of Samaria who was neither Jewish nor one of his own disciples. In this interaction Jesus provided his audience with a precedent for providing pastoral care even for those people who are outside the pastor's immediate community. Pastoral care is, therefore, an intentional, direct, immediate, spiritual, and existential response to the psychological, emotional, spiritual, and physical needs of people, regardless of whether they have accepted Jesus Christ as Lord and Savior.

When I was beginning my journey in the Christian ministry, one of my fathers in the ministry, Rev. Clarence James, taught me an adage that I value to this present day. He said, "It is difficult if not impossible to preach to a hungry stomach. If you feed the person first, they will be more likely to hear about the healing and salvific power of Jesus the Christ." Pastoral care represents the healing and transforming power of God's love for humanity (see John 3:16, *agape* love) within a specific time and place. Pastoral care takes seriously the notion that God's grace—unmerited love—is available to all who are in need of spiritual care.

The adjective *pastoral* is necessarily and forthrightly placed in front of the word *care* because (1) it denotes a type of care provided by the church, and (2) it is offered in the same protective and nurturing spirit that a shepherd provides to sheep. Pastoral care refers to various types of ministries within the church whether they are led by the pastor or by lay members of the congregation who are appointed by the pastor. As a direct response to the spiritual and existential needs of the congregation, pastoral care is often expressed within the church in a variety of ways. It may take the form of visitation by the deacons or notes of condolence from a bereavement committee; it may be expressed in a phone call from one member to another who has been absent from Sunday services or in a ministry to those who are homeless or incarcerated.

As clergy, we are called to be the spiritual shepherds of our congregants, and pastoral care represents both the theoretical and the theological arenas in which we show care and concern for our parishioners. We have a responsibility for providing the vision, the opportunities, the biblical teaching, and the role models for pastoral care, thereby encouraging all of our parishioners to participate in caring pastorally (as a shepherd for sheep) for their brothers and sisters in the body of Christ and in the world.

Pastoral care may occur outside of the walls of the local church, and it may concern individuals who are not members of the church. For example, a congregation might purchase a building located miles away from its sanctuary in an effort to establish a food bank or clothing exchange for needy residents of a nearby community. The primary goal of this ministry is to address the physical needs of the people, and a secondary goal may be to proclaim the good news of Jesus in word as well as deed. Even though the recipients of the ministry are not members of the church, the care that they receive from the pastor may be identified as pastoral. Jesus certainly did not know everyone in the crowd when he fed five thousand people with two fish and five loaves of bread (Matthew 14:13-21). Undoubtedly, as a result of the unexpected meal, some were inclined to learn more about the kingdom of heaven.

Some years ago I heard a sermon by Rev. Dr. Cecil Murray shortly after his retirement as the pastor of the First African Methodist Episcopal Church in Los Angeles. Within the course of his message Pastor Murray stated, "If we don't change the community, the community will corrupt the individual." I thought that his statement was profound, not just in the negative implications (an untransformed community has the power to corrupt individuals), but also for its positive ramifications (the church has the power to transform and redeem individuals).

Intentional pastoral care has the power to shape or reshape the community so that it will resemble the kingdom of heaven—what the Rev. Dr. Martin Luther King Jr. called "the beloved community." A ministry that intentionally avoids the process and goal of individual and social transformation has eluded the thrust and meaning of pastoral care. In fact, a ministry ceases to be pastoral in nature when the leadership of the ministry seeks to distance it from the mission of the church or when its impact seeks personal or monetary gain instead of the glorification of God. Effective pastoral care will always lead people to a greater understanding of the chief pastor and the good shepherd, Jesus the Christ.

2. The Meaning of Pastoral Counseling

Pastoral counseling is a specific type of pastoral care. It refers to the process by which pastors or pastoral caregivers (e.g., deacons, chaplains) seek to address the problems that confront individuals, couples, and families by using the techniques and insights provided by the social sciences and the Christian faith. Pastoral counseling is a discipline that reflects elements of art as well as science.

The art of pastoral counseling finds expression in the subjective aspects of the pastoral counselor's personality, style, and areas of expertise or personal experience. For example, the technique of one pastoral counselor may be heavily influenced by the twenty-seven books of the New Testament, whereas the technique of another pastoral counselor may emphasize the stories within the thirty-nine books of the Old Testament. One pastoral counselor may place an emphasis on the theology of *agape* love, while another pastoral counselor may explore the relational love (*philia*) that exists between the people seeking counsel. Some pastoral counselors specialize in counseling couples or families;

others may prefer working with seniors or youth. Most clergy find themselves counseling primarily parishioners from their own faith tradition, while other pastoral counselors (especially those who serve as chaplains) will function frequently in interfaith contexts. Some pastoral counselors may have expertise in counseling specific ethnic or cultural groups; others may have training in cross-cultural counseling. And of all these areas of expertise or preference, the art of pastoral counseling often emerges out of the personal experience or identity of the pastoral counselor.

In contrast, the science of pastoral counseling is rooted in the progress that scholars have made in understanding the body and mind from the perspectives of physiology, psychology, and other social sciences. For example, psychology provides pastoral counselors with a framework for understanding the tripartite structure of the human mind, which Freud identified as the id, ego, and superego. Psychology also assists pastoral counselors in understanding dynamics such as transference (the unconscious rapport between counselor and client) and countertransference.

The subjective-artistic and objective-scientific aspects of the pastoral counseling process help to shape the identity of the pastoral counselor and the context of the counseling session. Subsequent chapters will explore those factors and their significance for the counseling relationship, from issues of ethical boundaries to the integration of Christian principles and values in the counseling session.

3. Why People Turn to the Church

The well-known hymn "There's Not a Friend Like the Lowly Jesus" captures the faith that many people have in God's ability to help them with their hurts, challenges, and struggles. According to the lyricist, Johnson Oatman, "There's not a friend like the lowly Jesus: No, not one! No, not one! None else could heal all our soul's diseases: No, not one! No, not one!" People turn to the church in times of existential angst (environmental challenges), despair, and spiritual crises because they are looking for God to help and/or heal them.

Many of these people understand that psychologists and psychiatrists exist. Some distrust the wisdom of secular therapy; others may believe that only a Christian counselor has the remedy for the sin-sick soul. Others do not know where to begin or may not recognize the severity of their difficulties, and so they come first to the person they trust most: God's representative, their local pastor.

Whether these persons are faithful parishioners or seeking strangers to the church, they are expecting to find resources within the Christian tradition (e.g., prayer, fasting, and worship) that will help address their presenting problem. As clergy, we understand the power of God to help and to heal. In fact, we were all "old creatures" who became "new creatures" through Jesus Christ (2 Corinthians 5:17). Whether we are new to pastoral ministry or well seasoned in our vocation, clergy who desire to become competent pastoral counselors must explicitly recognize the solemn and sacred responsibility of making a covenant to provide pastoral care and counseling with a parishioner.

People come to the church for healing because they trust the pastoral counselor to act as a source of God's wisdom, compassion, healing, and accountability. Thus, the sacred covenant of pastoral counseling in a church setting goes beyond the important regulatory policies (e.g., code of ethics) of organizations such as the American Association of the Pastoral Counselors (AAPC) and the American Psychiatric Association (APA) and the code of conduct for ministers explicitly stated in the doctrine and discipline of most mainline denominations. We are accountable for representing both the transcendent wisdom and the immanent compassion of our God to the people of God, especially those who may have never before encountered the gospel or its messengers.

It is worth recalling here that pastoral counselors are, of course, human beings. We have flaws of our own; we are very much "wounded healers," and that reality will eventually surface in our counseling sessions and relationships. Wayne Oates, a brilliant author and professor in the area of practical theology, wrote a book titled *When Religion Gets Sick*. Throughout the book Oates discusses the relationship between religion and psychopathology, which he refers to as "sickness."[1] A host of factors (environmental and genetic) produce pathological behaviors, and the church is not exempt from those sicknesses. Nor are we as church leaders invulnerable. In chapter 4 below, I discuss how the pathology of a counselor can affect the counseling relationship. For now, it is sufficient to acknowledge that despite the imperfections of even faithful pastoral counselors, people continue to turn to the church for hope and healing. And for those individuals, the pastoral counseling session is one of the few arenas in which authentic hope and healing may occur in the local church.

4. Pastoral Identity and Christian Values

Clergy who are serving as pastor of a church necessarily have a variety of roles to fulfill. At times a preacher, at times a Bible study leader, at times an evangelist who reaches beyond the local congregation with the gospel message, the pastor is also an administrator who supervises the church staff and ministry leaders. And of course, at some point in parish ministry the pastor will be called on to function as pastoral counselor.

These diverse and sometimes competing roles often become challenging for one person to manage. In such circumstances the pastor may need to meet with the pastoral relations committee (or similar group) and discuss priorities and expectations. That discernment process may result in identifying certain tasks and responsibilities that can be delegated or eliminated without negatively affecting the spiritual health and growth of the church. It is my conviction that pastoral counseling is not a task that can be delegated or eliminated. It is too vital to the broader responsibility of pastoral care, without which the vitality of the congregation will suffer. Therefore, the role of pastoral counselor is integral to the identity of the local church pastor.

The term *identity* concerns the psychological concept of self and its relation to others. The sense of self emerges from biological factors as well as from environmental influences, and as people of faith, we affirm that each person's sense of self is uniquely informed by that person's relationship with God. These three sources—biological, environmental, and relational with God—contribute to the unique formation of every human being's concept of self.

For example, biology contributes factors including, but not limited to, gender, race, physical health and ability, sexuality, and intelligence. Environment shapes our natural personality and adds layers of social conditioning and cultural values related to gender, race, ability, age, and socioeconomic class, as well as contributing the influences of nurture, education, and personal experience. Each individual's relationship with God, whether as an atheist, agnostic, or devout practitioner of a particular faith, will further influence how that individual relates to the world, to people, to other living creatures, and to self. Never have we been more aware of these complex and diverse realities than in this postmodern generation of the twenty-first century.

The goal of pastoral counseling is to help parishioners claim a healthy sense of self. That may mean acknowledging and addressing weaknesses or illnesses, tending to spiritual or psychological wounds, or learning to accept and embrace certain aspects of self that have been devalued, abused, or otherwise rejected by the individual or by others. In other words, to facilitate that process in their parishioners, pastoral counselors must initiate that process for themselves. For that rea-

son, it is strongly recommended that the pastoral counselor meet the following requirements:

■ Complete a formal course in the area of pastoral
counseling, its theory and practice, preferably in a seminary or graduate school context.

■ Seek pastoral counseling from a qualified pastoral
counselor who can introduce the process and facilitate
it in the aspiring candidate.

■ Continue regular self-assessments and self-analysis
throughout ministry, recognizing that the complex biological, environmental, and relational factors are
dynamic and continual in their ongoing contributions
to the ever-developing sense of self.

The pastor who does not explore and critically
examine issues of his or her own identity prior to
attempting pastoral counseling for others will
inevitably impose an incoherent, conflicted, or fragmented sense of self into the counseling experience.

Let me be clear: I am not suggesting that the pastor
create a "perfect self" or even attempt to project that
to a parishioner. As human beings, pastors are inherently and inescapably flawed, being in constant need of
the healing, cleansing, and guiding power of the Holy
Spirit. As pastoral counselors, we are wounded healers
at our core. However, we have a solemn and sacred

responsibility to offer the best possible pastoral counsel, and that requires that we be sufficiently self-aware
so as not to inflict our own wounds on anyone else.
Our journey toward the ideal of excellence in pastoral
counseling involves the courage to identify, embrace,
and possibly change aspects of ourselves that may
thwart the human and divine potential of the parishioners whom we love and are called to serve.

5. Establishing the Context for Pastoral Counseling

Generally speaking, the ideal setting for pastoral counseling is both private and professional. Most pastors
prefer to meet with individuals or couples in their
church office, where parishioners have the comfort of
proximity to the sanctuary, the relative comfort of an
office setting, and the assurance of confidentiality
behind closed doors. This ideal setting includes chairs
arranged in an intimate grouping, facing one another,
with sufficient lighting and a moderate climate to allow
for maximum comfort, as well as a time when inter-
ruptions may be controlled or otherwise avoided.

This ideal setting is designed to address the following needs of the pastoral counseling session
and relationship:

■ Time and space to ask questions and listen to the answers in order to learn as much as possible about the parishioner and the presenting problem

■ Privacy to reassure any concerns about the session being kept confidential

■ Minimal distractions so as to facilitate open communication, honest reactions, thoughtful responses, and creative strategies for moving forward

That is the ideal. In reality, however, pastoral counseling often transpires in a variety of settings. A chance meeting in the church parking lot or hallway, an emergency phone call from a distraught member, a rushed appearance at a house fire or vehicle accident, a visit to the intensive care unit at a local hospital or the grief-darkened home of a bereaved family—all these and more may become the pastor's initial encounter with a person in need of pastoral counseling. In critical moments the pastoral counselor will surrender the ideal and respond to the situation to the best of his or her ability, trying to be mindful of pragmatic considerations such as privacy and boundaries while also offering the compassionate and attentive response that the parishioner so desperately needs.

These diverse and spontaneous circumstances will give way in subsequent counseling encounters to other complexities, which vary in relation to the individual parishioner, the present problem, and other persons or groups involved. These present a series of challenges for the pastor who is trying to establish a coherent, professional, and supportive context for pastoral counseling. Even when the ideal physical setting of the pastor's private office is attainable, the ideal relational context for the counseling encounter often remains elusive.

According to Charles Gerkin, people are "living human documents,"[2] and in a real sense the pastoral counselor's task is to listen to the parishioner's story and help that person to rewrite his or her personal narrative in a transforming and healing way. Establishing a professional context of pastoral counseling enables the pastor to conduct an initial interview with the parishioner, provide an overview of the counseling process, and help the parishioner to understand the parameters of the healing process before it begins. In this safe and formalized context the parishioner has the opportunity to explore an experience that has been confusing, disorienting, shocking, and painful, and the pastor has a professional framework within which to undertake psychological assessment and theological reflection over a period of time.

As a teenager, I earned money each summer by painting houses. I quickly learned to look at an exterior or a room and estimate the hours required to paint it. What I frequently underestimated was the time required to prepare a surface for painting. I discovered the need to factor in molding to be taped, furniture to be moved, and floors to be covered. The prep work was often far more complex and time-consuming than the painting itself. The same can be said of our work as pastoral counselors. The process of preparing to engage in pastoral counseling with a parishioner is as important as, and often more challenging than, the actual process of pastoral care and counseling. Therefore, the following section is intended to provide new and seasoned clergy with a brief overview of the process for establishing the formal context for pastoral counseling.

The First Session

What type of questions should the pastoral counselor ask at the outset of the counseling relationship? Most pastoral counselors make use of a standard intake form to collect preliminary and introductory information about the parishioner who is seeking counsel. This form may be provided to the parishioner in the waiting area prior to commencing the first session, or it may be completed by the pastoral counselor in conversation with the parishioner during that initial session. In addition to routine information such as name, age, vocation, marital or family status, and contact information, the form can address pragmatic questions concerning fees (if any), health insurance (if applicable), and the length and number of sessions. (The specific categories of a basic intake form are discussed in more detail in chapter 18 of this book.)

Perhaps most critically, however, the form should include questions that pertain to the parishioner's clinical, medical, and environmental history. For example, what antidepressants have been prescribed for the parishioner, and how regularly are those medications being taken? Is the parishioner currently under the care of a psychiatrist? If so, will the parishioner consent to allowing the pastoral counselor to share his or her notes with the primary clinical caregiver in order to provide a holistic web of care? Any and all such information is confidential and written documentation of the sessions should be kept under lock and key. The only exceptions to this strict and sacred ethic of confidentiality are (1) if the parishioner has a plan to commit suicide, and (2) if he or she is currently abusing a minor. In such special instances, in most states, the pastoral counselor has a legal obligation to report that information immediately to the proper authorities (police, parents, social services, etc.).

Overall, the pastoral counselor should be mindful about framing the questions in this initial session in a sensitive and compassionate manner. Pastoral counseling should not be understood as a coercive and intrusive process. It is a voluntary and relational experience in which the bond of trust that already exists between pastor and parishioner might be strengthened and deepened. Therefore, any initial assessment, be it on paper or in person, should not be used to poke or prod the parishioner. Establish the formal counseling session as a warm, safe, and welcoming context where the counselor forms a covenant relationship with the parishioner who is experiencing some type of spiritual crisis in order to provide the advice, counsel, comfort, and faith that are desperately needed.

Planning the Counseling Session

Parishioners seeking pastoral counseling may contact the church office to schedule an appointment, or they may make direct contact with the pastor. If possible, the pastor should establish a particular time and day for regular counseling sessions. For family counseling, the pastoral counselor may offer to meet in the home of the parishioners. The home environment is reassuring and comforting, especially if the counseling session is centered on the death of a family member, but also when children are involved. When counseling individuals, however, I suggest sessions that occur at the church office during regular business hours. If a parishioner can meet only on Saturday, I recommend scheduling sessions when other people are present in the building. The content of the counseling session is necessarily confidential, but for the safety of both pastor and parishioner, it is best for the church secretary or pastor's administrative assistant to be aware that a private meeting is occurring in the church.

Begin each session by greeting the parishioner with a handshake, not a kiss or a hug. Physical contact with a parishioner during the pastoral counseling session may be construed as sexual misconduct, particularly when the presenting problem is related to sexual issues. According to Ronald Bullis and Cynthia Mazur, "Sexual contact is becoming synonymous with misconduct. Nine states have determined that sexual contact with a counselee is a criminal act by the therapist."[3] Even though pastoral counseling in the church context is typically a free service offered as part of the clergy's pastoral care, the pastoral counselor is still liable for how he or she treats the client prior to and during the therapeutic encounter.[4]

6. Faith as the Final Factor

To be a Christian is to be a witness God's revelatory, healing, consistent, and awesome power along the journey of life. To be a pastoral counselor is to witness the aforementioned attributes of God within the life of the parishioner and/or person seeking pastoral counseling. Throughout this section I have discussed the essential elements of an awareness of the pastor's identity, a sense of clinical competence, a comprehensive intake form, and an understanding of the difference between pastoral care and pastoral counseling. However, I have failed to mention how the theological virtue of faith is essential to the success of the pastoral counselor as well as the counselee.

Even though the weekly pastoral counseling sessions should not exceed four months—a relatively brief period of time—it is understood that the pastoral counselor has faith in God's ability to help or heal the client, faith in his or her own skill level or professional competence, and faith in the parishioner who desires to achieve the goals established in counseling. Ultimately, it will not be the idea of identity or competence that threatens to derail the pastoral counseling process; it is a crisis of faith that can thwart the process at the outset. If the pastoral counselor does not believe in the life-changing, miraculous power of God to intervene in human affairs and positively influence the clinical process, the pastoral counseling session may be doomed from the beginning. The pastoral counselor must affirm, initially within himself or herself and then with the parishioner, that God has the ability to help and heal this person.

Within the first four or five sessions the pastoral counselor may hear stories of abuse, neglect, addiction, bereavement, bankruptcy, unemployment, homeless-ness, incest, or divorce. These stories may challenge the belief system of the pastoral counselor and counselee. If a temporary crisis in faith occurs at the outset of the session, the pastoral counselor may need to pray the prayer of the father who brought his tormented son to Jesus: "I believe; help my unbelief" (Mark 9:24).

Notes

1. *A Practical Handbook for Ministry: From the Writings of Wayne E. Oates*, ed. Thomas W. Chapman (Louisville: Westminster/John Knox Press, 1992), 437.

2. Charles V. Gerkin, *The Living Human Document: Re-Visioning Pastoral Counseling in a Hermeneutical Mode* (Nashville: Abingdon Press, 1984), 40.

3. Ronald K. Bullis and Cynthia S. Mazur, *Legal Issues and Religious Counseling* (Louisville: Westminster/John Knox Press, 1993), 107.

4. Ibid., 3.

Pastoral Counseling in Context

7. Pastoral Counseling and the Postmodern Endeavor

Postmodernity has been defined a number of different ways, some more accessible than others.[1] For our purposes here, let it suffice to say that the term *postmodern* refers to a philosophical, as opposed to theological, position that seeks to give expression and authority to the unique aspects of the self as they are expressed within the context of culture, race, class, gender, and sexual orientation. Postmodernity essentially maintains that a person's social location (e.g., one's status or position in the United States of America) will produce a distinct set of experiences for that individual; therefore, the insights gained from those experiences produce a "way of knowing" for the individual within his or her social location. This postmodern way of knowing represents a kind of truth that may seem alarmingly subjective and fluid to those accustomed to the fixed, external view of truth in the earlier modern era.

What significance does this aspect of postmodernity have for clergy in the context of pastoral counseling? On the constructive side, postmodernity has given expression, hope, authority, and legitimacy to groups of people who have been historically marginalized and alienated by those within the mainstream of the American experience. At the same time, the postmodern perspective challenges the church's traditional conviction that all members of society are called to embrace an ideal Christian worldview and value system. In other words, a pastoral counselor who attempts to counsel a postmodern parishioner to conform to the ethical or moral code of the church may encounter resistance. Not only is much of the church's love ethic contrary to the present-day American values of individualism and materialism, but also the idea that a single answer is sufficient for all people, regardless of culture, class, or gender identity, may seem ludicrous. Parishioners who live in a postmodern culture are necessarily shaped by the ideals of an increasingly diverse and complex secular society; and in that postmodern culture each person is empowered to shape his or her own value system in response to unique personal experiences.

As a result, the pastoral counseling session may become an arena where significant culture clash occurs. In such a session the pastoral counselor represents an authority figure (which makes him or her suspect in a post-Watergate, post–clergy sexual abuse generation). And that authority figure is often perceived as offering naïve answers from ancient Scriptures too often used to abuse, oppress, or exploit. Even for a parishioner within the church who does embrace a Christian worldview and traditional values, a postmodern culture clash may occur based on identity alone. For example, someone with a postmodern perspective may think that it is impossible for a middle-class, white Anglo-Saxon Protestant (WASP), male pastor to understand or counsel an impoverished, unchurched, African American female who is suffering the effects of sexism and racism.

This section is specifically dedicated to helping pastoral counselors (1) identify the potential conflict between postmodernity and the traditional claims made by the church, (2) see the inherent value of the Christian perspective within the often fragmented and ever-changing postmodern landscape, and (3) determine the extent to which the gulf between church and culture can, should, and must be bridged within the pastoral counseling session. The advent of globalization has assisted in the promotion of a postmodern perspective throughout the global community. If the church in general and pastoral counselors in particular are to going to be relevant in the lives of people who live within this postmodern milieu, then the values espoused by proponents of postmodernity must be identified, evaluated, and then either challenged or embraced within the pastoral counseling session so that people may have a deeper appreciation for God in general and the love of Christ in particular as it exists within a universal community of faith.

8. The Countercultural Mission of the Church

The church is an institution that is tasked with keeping alive the teachings and rituals of Jesus the Christ. One may argue that the mission of the church is recorded in the Great Commission: "Go therefore and make disciples of all nations, baptizing them in the name of the Father and of the Son and of the Holy Spirit, and teaching them to obey everything that I have commanded you. And remember, I am with you always, to the end of the age" (Matthew 28:19-20). Jesus, the Son of God, also instructed his disciples to follow the commands of Scripture, "'You shall love the Lord your God with all your heart, and with all your soul, and with all your mind'" (Matthew 22:37), adding, "'You shall love your neighbor as yourself.' On these two commandments hang all the law and the prophets" (Matthew 22:39-40).

Jesus clearly identified love as the ethical norm by which all human actions should be considered blameworthy or praiseworthy. The mission of the church is to spread the gospel (good news) of Jesus the Christ while telling others about God's love for humankind. Within this context of love for God and love for one's neighbor, Jesus and Paul list and elaborate upon the thoughts and actions that are considered blameworthy and praiseworthy from a Christian perspective. In other words, Jesus, Paul, and other biblical writers sought to interpret the divine principles of love, grace, and justice in the context of human experience and culture. Whether their topic was the Sabbath, marriage and divorce, slavery, or household relationships, they were attempting to establish a culture in the early church that was distinct in many ways from the Jewish, Greek, and Roman cultures of the day.

The mission of the church remains countercultural inasmuch as our values may often be in conflict with the dominant values of an inherently secular culture, in which we currently exist. While it is conceivable that postmodern parishioners may categorically reject

Jesus' notion of an unconditional and universal love ethic, it is more likely that they will disagree with Jesus' stated position regarding "acceptable" grounds for divorce, or Paul's views on sexual relationships. So, how might a pastoral counselor advise the parishioner who is seeking a divorce because of trauma rooted in a history of domestic violence? How does a pastoral counselor approach a young couple seeking premarital counseling in order to address the complex dynamics of a relationship in which they are already sexually active and in fact may have a child? What about the homosexual son of a recently deceased church member—a young man who desperately needs counseling help in dealing with his grief? The pastoral counselor will need to be prayerful and diligent in applying Jesus' love ethic to interpret both biblical texts and cultural trends in relevant and compassionate ways.

The tension between Christian and cultural values will not be exclusively moral. Consider how a Caucasian pastoral counselor might respond to an African American parishioner who has difficulty trusting someone whose skin color stirs up deep pain about racist wounds of the past. What about the engaged couple who are equal in education and career status and who question traditional church teachings about

Paul's views on gender roles in marriage? What about a young entrepreneur who discloses business practices that pursue profits at the expense of personal integrity or the welfare and dignity of others?

The empowering but fragmented, liberating but subjective, authoritative but parochial perspectives of these parishioners have found their way into the storefront as well as the megachurches of the world. Through the art of listening the pastoral counselor endeavors to form a "dialogical bridge of understanding" between the values of postmodernity and those of the church. While some cultural values will ultimately be identified by the pastoral counselor and the parishioner as mutually exclusive to the values of Christ and his church, it is to be hoped that the pastor (who is also a product of the postmodern culture) will find ways to communicate the hope, life, and power of God's love even in the midst of cultural tensions. Even if the counselor and parishioner agree to end the counseling relationship after the initial therapeutic encounter, the parting may be one of benediction and blessing if carried out within the framework of God's universal love for humankind.

The *agape* love ethic of Jesus the Christ should always serve as the ethical norm within the session; therefore, the humanity or personhood of the postmodern parishioner, who is necessarily a child of God, should never be rejected, alienated, or dismissed because of the postmodern values that become evident within the pastoral counseling session. The following sections offer suggestions that may assist pastors in addressing the categories of gender, race, class, and sexual orientation during the pastoral counseling session. Inasmuch as pastoral counseling is both an art as well as a science, a cookie-cutter approach to pastoral counseling with the postmodern parishioner does not exist. However, insights from psychologists, theologians, cultural critics, public intellectuals, and therapists have been helpful in an overall effort to construct a coherent theory of pastoral counseling.

9. Pastoral Counseling and Women

In order to identify and embrace a comprehensive and effective model of pastoral care and counseling for women, I believe that the pastoral counselor must embrace a "theology of mutuality." A theology of mutuality necessarily affirms the inherent worth and value of women in general and women seeking pastoral counseling in general by embracing the principle that God created men and women to be equals within and outside of the pastoral counseling session.

It is not difficult to locate books and articles written by ministers and theologians that seek to devalue the ontology (being), praxis (action), and experience of women as they have found expression in the church, academy, and civic and cultural institutions. Within the church some male ministers have used passages of Scripture to objectivize and demonize women. There are still denominations that prohibit women from becoming licensed and ordained clergy, leaving them unable to realize or fulfill their calling within the local congregation. When pastors fail to place women in positions of authority within the local church, pastors or denominational leadership may be making a value judgment with regard to the value of women in the congregation.

A theology of mutuality rejects all claims of an inherent male superiority within a congregation. A theology of mutuality affirms God's love for both men and women and maintains that there should be no power differentials based on gender within the church. A theology of mutuality views sexism within and outside of the church as a manifestation of sin that necessarily contributes to a breach in our human relationship with God. A theology of mutuality affirms the presence of different roles within the church; however, it maintains that these roles are not a result of the gender distinctions between men and women.

A successful pastoral counseling session between a male or a female counselor and a female counselee will necessarily be rooted in a theology of mutuality. If a pastoral counselor is unable to affirm the inherent worth of the female parishioner seeking pastoral counseling, which is a necessity based on God's understanding and value of persons, then the pastoral counselor should make a referral to another pastoral counselor who is willing and able to affirm the parishioner's worth. The theory and the theology of pastoral counseling necessarily precede its practices within the local church; therefore, it is essential that the theology that undergirds the pastoral counseling session with the postmodern female parishioner be rooted in a theology that affirms both her humanity and her identity.

The pastoral counselor who seeks to provide pastoral counseling to women should not assume that the woman in the present counseling session has issues, challenges, or conflicts that are similar to the woman client in the preceding session or the woman client in the next. Women are not a monolithic group, and a diversity of expression necessarily exists among them, as does also a diversity of issues that will be confronted in pastoral counseling. Therefore, the pastoral counselor should not view a counseling session with one woman as normative; rather, the counselor should strive to identify commonalties among the narratives of women parishioners and strive to develop a technique that will help these parishioners to identify and resolve their presenting problem.

Lastly, the pastoral counselor must be sensitive to the issue of gender-exclusive language during the pastoral counseling sessions. For example, many pastors use the pronoun "he" in reference to God because Jesus said, for example, "Our Father in heaven" (Matthew 6:9). However, constant use of the pronoun "he" in reference to God for a woman parishioner who has been the victim of domestic abuse may impede her ability to reach her goals in pastoral counseling. In short, the pastoral counselor should be careful about using heavily masculine images of God, as well as choosing Scripture passages, exegetical commentary, or any hermeneutic that implicitly or explicitly devalues women or exacerbates their presenting problem. I recommend *God in Her Midst: Preaching Healing to Wounded Women* by Elaine Flake (Judson Press, 2006) for parishioners as well as pastoral counselors who are interested in ministering with greater sensitivity to women. Pastoral counseling should be a healing, liberating, and empowering experience for women, and the counselor must take great care to help facilitate these desirable ends.

10. Pastoral Counseling and African Americans

Historically, African Americans have been a victimized population. Since African Americans have experienced pain, anger, violence, dread, fear, and hatred from people and institutions because of the color of their skin, there are pastors, psychologists, and theologians in the field of pastoral care and counseling who believe that the concept of race should be explicitly addressed throughout the process of the counseling sessions of African American clients if they are to have any success in reaching their established goals.

One recognized African American psychologist, Archie Smith, author of *Navigating the Deep River: Spirituality in African American Families*, does not argue that African American clients must receive counseling exclusively from African American therapists in order for the clients to achieve their goals; however, he does maintain that counselors seeking to successfully treat African American clients must have a knowledge of African American history and culture. The counselor must also seek to understand the manner in which systemic and institutional racism has affected the African American self and has manifested itself in society.

Providing pastoral counseling to African American parishioners can also be viewed and understood within the larger context of cross-cultural counseling. According to David Augsburger, "Clinical skills within a culture are not sufficient. Cultural skills that transcend and thus can participate in transforming culture are equally crucial."[2] For example, a white, Protestant, male pastoral counselor who is providing counseling to a black (e.g., from Zimbabwe), Catholic female who recently arrived in the United States must be prepared to evaluate his assumption with regard to Western individualism, the structure of the family unit, capitalism, and democracy. The pastoral counselor must strive to understand the parishioner's cultural ideas before imposing his or her values onto the parishioner or the counseling session. The pastoral counselor should not assume that the parishioner is African American simply because he or she is black. In short, the pastoral counselor must strive to understand his or her own political, economic, cultural, and religious value system as well as that of the black or African American client if the goals of the counseling session are to be achieved by the client.

Smith's critical analysis of African American culture has implications for pastoral counselors seeking to work with African American parishioners. In many ways, the goals of the Civil Rights movement have been achieved, culminating in the election of a black man, Barack Obama, to the most powerful political office in the United States of America. However, one may still speak of a particular segment of African American culture that has been negatively impacted by failing public school systems and disproportionate rates of incarceration, substance abuse, AIDS diagnoses, teenage pregnancy, unemployment and underemployment, and illiteracy.

It is difficult if not impossible to determine the extent to which historical oppression continues to have an effect on contemporary African American life. Nevertheless, pastoral counselors who desire to work with certain segments of the African American population will have more success if they strive to understand what Cornel West calls the "nihilist threat" to the black community. According to West, the nihilistic threat "is primarily a question of speaking to the profound sense of psychological depression, personal worthlessness, and social despair so widespread in black America."[3] In short, the nihilistic threat refers to the negative values that harmfully impact black life, and these may manifest themselves in the pastoral counseling session.

Edward Wimberly presents a strategy that has proven to be effective in addressing segments of this nihilist threat as it appears in pastoral counseling sessions with African American clients. Wimberly argues that these negative values, and the perspectives that African Americans have about themselves, will be understood when the pastoral counselor seeks to listen to and edit the narrative of the client. Wimberly states, "From a narrative perspective, pastoral care can be defined as bringing all the resources of the faith story into the context of caring relationships, to bear upon the lives of people as they face life struggles which are personal, interpersonal, and emotional."[4] The pastoral counselor who has helped the African American client to "reauthor" this personal narrative will also be expected to help the parishioner to resolve his or her conflicts and relieve the anxiety that may be leading to a dysfunctional professional or personal life.

11. Pastoral Counseling and the Poor

Pastoral counseling with postmodern parishioners takes seriously the notion that people of all socioeconomic levels are in need of spiritual guidance to overcome personal, familial, and environmental problems. It is not uncommon to locate a megachurch with thousands of members and a multimillion-dollar budget in many of the larger cities throughout the United States. However, most congregations in both metropolitan and rural areas throughout the United States have neither thousands of members on their rolls nor millions of dollars in their budgets. These churches are composed primarily of working-class members, and many of them have at least one ministry or event (e.g., food pantry, clothing bank, prison ministry, free health screenings) dedicated to helping the poor.

In Matthew 26:11 Jesus told his disciples that the poor will always be with us. In an effort to demonstrate the love of Christ to this demographic, pastors have designed and funded pastoral care and counseling programs in churches throughout the nation. Some parishioners who live below the poverty line have made poor decisions that have resulted in their current economic condition, while other parishioners are the unfortunate victims of a generational cycle of poverty. A third group of impoverished parishioners are the unfortunate victims of extenuating circumstances such as unemployment, underemployment, divorce, and bankruptcy.

It is essential for those who are looking to embrace a comprehensive model of pastoral care and counseling with the poor to refrain from passing judgment on those who are poor and in need of pastoral care and counseling. The pastoral counselor must recognize the fact that the roles of the pastoral counselor and the impoverished parishioner could have been reversed if the pastoral counselor were subjected to the tragedies and extenuating circumstances that confronted the parishioner. In fact, the pastoral counselor may soon discover that he or she has more in common with the impoverished parishioner than their initial encounter might suggest. The pastoral counselor should recognize the humanity and divine potential of the impoverished parishioner prior to beginning the process of assessment. An inclusive theology that seeks to affirm the self-worth and value of those who are poor must undergird any model or technique associated with pastoral care and counseling.

Nancy Boyd-Franklin, professor of applied and professional psychology at Rutgers University, provides a methodology for engaging in the lives of poor families. Her knowledge of the church as well as a social and psychological understanding of the issues that affect poor black families have implications for pastoral counselors seeking to provide counseling to parishioners.[5] Inasmuch as many impoverished individuals and families within the church are involved with institutions such as departments of correction, mental health facilities, public schools, departments of social services, departments of child welfare, Alcoholics Anonymous, Narcotics Anonymous, and transitional care facilities, the pastoral counselor must assume the role of "systems guide" in order to address the intrapersonal as well as existential concerns of these individuals and families who are poor.

The use of assessment tools such as a genogram, which will be discussed in detail in chapter 28, will assist the pastoral counselor in identifying the systems that are positively impacting (e.g., the church) and negatively impacting (e.g., family members who necessarily contribute to the parishioner's anxiety) the impoverished parishioner's psychological, social, and spiritual development. The pastoral counselor may have to make telephone calls (with the written consent of the parishioner) to these agencies as well as make personal appearances at these institutions (e.g., schools and the courts) in order to assist the impoverished parishioner through the maze of institutions. The pastoral counselor may have to assume the role of spiritual advisor, therapist, social worker, and case manager. At the very least, the pastoral counselor must be intimately involved with a secular team that is attempting to provide holistic care to the impoverished individual or family.

12. Pastoral Counseling and the LGBTQ Community

The subject of homosexuality is a controversial one in the church. I have written this section with the understanding that pastoral counseling with people who are lesbian, gay, bisexual, transgender, or questioning in their sexual orientation (LGBTQ) can and should take place. However, I also understand that providing pastoral counseling to members of the LGBTQ community may be a particularly challenging endeavor for heterosexual pastoral counselors who have embraced the traditional view of Judeo-Christian ethics. Therefore, I have written this section specifically for heterosexual, new, and seasoned clergy who see LGBTQ people as God's children and in some way want to bring hope and healing in their lives.

For pastoral counselors who believe that Scripture prohibits homosexual behavior as sinful, the prospect of counseling a person who openly self-identifies as LGBTQ ("Q" referring those who are "questioning," their identity) is likely to present a true moral and ethical dilemma. However, I believe that it is possible to provide pastoral counseling to members of the LGBTQ community even if the pastoral counselor has embraced a traditional position with regard to sexual ethics in the Christian church.

God loves people. John 3:16 reminds us, "God so loved the world that he gave his only Son, so that everyone who believes in him may not perish but may have eternal life." It is abundantly clear that God does not love all that we do, for each and every one of us sometimes engages in sinful thoughts and actions. However, God does not withdraw God's love or grace from us, and through the process of confession, repentance, and forgiveness we are restored into a right relationship with God. Members of the LGBTQ community are people first and LGBTQ second. As people, they are capable of loving God and loving their neighbors as they love themselves. They are also capable of receiving love from others in general and pastoral counselors in particular. Marie Fortune states, "Love does no harm to another. If I am seeking to love another person, I can best begin by trying not to do harm to that person."[6] Pastoral counseling with LGBTQ parishioners begins with (1) recognizing that they are people loved by God, and (2) striving to do no harm to them by exacerbating their presenting problem, ignoring a possible intrapersonal or intrapsychic conflict, or using the pastoral counseling moment to further their guilt or shame. Preaching and counseling are two distinct acts. Preaching is primarily proclaiming, and counseling is primarily listening, unraveling, and suggesting. It is through the process of counseling that parishioners can reach goals that assist them in becoming functional in their personal and professional lives.

As people, members of the LGBTQ community may want to talk in pastoral counseling sessions about issues other than their intimate relationships. For example, they may want to discuss their grief over losing a parent, their addition to alcohol, or their anger with their boss, probation officer, or child. A competent and caring pastoral counselor who believes that sex between a man and woman outside of the confines of marriage is sinful will still be willing and able to help the LGBTQ parishioner to process these issues without entering into a discussion about sexual ethics. He or she will quickly recognize that people are made in the image of God (*imago Dei*) and will be eager to serve God's people through the process of counseling.

If the pastoral counselor (1) believes that everyone except members of the LGBTQ community were made in the image of God, (2) tends to limit or reduce the totality of the human experience to one's sexual orientation, or (3) intends to hurt, harm, or punish LGBTQ parishioners by exacerbating their shame, guilt, anxiety, or conflict that may or may not be related to sexual orientation, then the pastoral counselor should not attempt to provide counseling to LGBTQ parishioners. It is possible for a LGBTQ parishioner to be harmed, as opposed to helped, during a pastoral counseling session.

Depending on the evolving dynamics of the pastoral counseling session, the pastoral counselor may have an ethical obligation to state his or her theological position on sexual ethics and refer the LGBTQ parishioner to another pastoral counselor if necessary. Ultimately, the goal of pastoral counseling is to improve the lives of people who are seeking help from that process. It is possible to provide meaningful spiritual and clinical care to members of the LGBTQ community; however, meaningful care will occur only if pastoral counselors are candid, transparent, and reflective about their own identity, theology, and understanding of persons in need.

13. Measuring Success in Pastoral Counseling

Success in pastoral counseling is measured by the parishioner's ability to (1) achieve insight regarding the nature of his or her presenting problem, and (2) refrain from irrational or negative thoughts and dysfunctional behavior as he or she reaches and practices the goals that were conceived during the pastoral counseling sessions. The goals that are to be achieved by the parishioner should be goals that are constructed by the pastoral counselor as well as the parishioner (e.g., sobriety).

If a pastoral counselor does not believe that he or she will be instrumental in helping a certain segment of "postmodern parishioners" (e.g., persons of a different race, ethnicity, socioeconomic class, gender, or sexual orientation) achieve mutually established goals in counseling, then the counselor should refrain from providing counseling to such persons and make a referral. In order for a parishioner to be helped in pastoral counseling sessions, the counselor must address his or her own biases, fears, anxieties, conflicts, and overall ignorance in working with different types of people. If the pastoral counselor refuses to address these issues through honest self-examination, the parishioner may be hurt or made worse by the pastoral counseling that he or she receives. People have prejudices, shortcomings, and biases; therefore, new and seasoned clergy who are interested in providing pastoral counseling will have their own prejudices, shortcomings, and biases. An introspective examination of these biases will greatly enhance the ability of the pastoral counselor to provide counseling to postmodern parishioners.

Notes

1. Cornel West, professor at Princeton University and Union Seminary, has described postmodernity in these terms: "Yet neither the popular nor the academic

mind—given the relative lack of a historical sense of both—fully grasp the major determinants of postmodern culture: the unprecedented impact of market forces on everyday life, including the academy and the art world, the displacement of Europe by America in regard to global cultural influence (and imitation), and the increase of political polarization in cultural affairs by national, racial, gender, and sexual orientation, especially within the highly bureaucratized world of ideas and opinions" (Cornel West, *Prophetic Reflections: Notes on Race and Power in America* [Monroe, ME: Common Courage Press, 1993]), 39).

2. David W. Augsburger, *Pastoral Counseling across Cultures* (Philadelphia: Westminster, 1986), 20.

3. Cornel West, *Race Matters* (New York: Vintage Books, 1994), 20.

4. Edward P. Wimberly, *African American Pastoral Care* (Nashville: Abingdon Press, 1991), 18.

5. See, for example, Nancy Boyd-Franklin, *Black Families in Therapy: Understanding the African American Experience*, 2nd ed. (New York: Guilford Press, 2003).

6. Marie M. Fortune, *Love Does No Harm: Sexual Ethics for the Rest of Us* (New York: Continuum, 1995), 34.

The Tasks of Pastoral Counseling

14. A Biblical Foundation

Jesus was regarded as the Great Physician. Many instances in the Gospel narratives detail the accounts in which Jesus saw people with physical limitations (e.g., blindness, leprosy, inability to walk) and healed them. His obvious, earnest, and intentional concern for the physical well-being of people who may or may not have embraced his message about the kingdom of God was explicitly manifested in the miracles that occurred among these people. The Gospels also reveal that Jesus' ability to help and heal was not limited to the physical well-being of the people with whom he came into contact. By saying "Your sins are forgiven....Stand up and walk" (Matthew 9:5), Jesus is making a statement that has theological as well as psychological implications: the individual has been restored to a right relationship with God, and the individual's anxiety has been relieved through the cathartic and healing experience of forgiveness.

Jesus also attempted to help his followers by addressing all of their needs—psychological, emotional, and spiritual. He sought to relieve their psychological anxiety with the statement "Do not let not your hearts be troubled" (John 14:1). The biblical record also contains an instance in which Peter was experiencing a spiritual crisis of faith. When Peter, who was walking on water, took his eyes off of Jesus, he began to sink. Jesus addressed and helped Peter to resolve his faith crisis (Matthew 14:22-33). Throughout his three-year public ministry Jesus helped to resolve emotional crises ("Why do you make a commotion and weep? The child is not dead but sleeping" [Mark 5:39]), physical challenges (a blind man's sight was restored [John 9:1-7]), and struggles of faith ("Ask, and it will be given you; search, and you will find; knock, and the door will be opened for you" [Matthew 7:7]). Prior to helping the people in the Gospel narrative, Jesus conducted an assessment of their respective problems. The methods by which Jesus conducted his diagnosis are not always explicitly stated in the biblical record. However, the intent of his diagnosis and the resulting treatment plan are abundantly clear: he loved people and wanted them to be helped or healed so that they, as well as others, would be more inclined to enter into a new covenant or new relationship with God.

The life and ministry of Jesus as the Great Physician can serve as a theological point of departure for pastoral counselors who are tasked with the responsibility of helping parishioners to resolve cognitive, behavioral, and spiritual problems that are presented in typical pastoral counseling sessions. This section is intended to help pastoral counselors continue to embrace Jesus' model for helping people, a model that will enable the pastoral counselor to better diagnose and resolve the problems presented in the pastoral counseling sessions. This section presupposes that (1) Jesus' model of healing people for the purpose of helping them to gain a closer relationship with God is still relevant in this generation and culture, and that (2) the theoretical insights, assessment tools, and resulting treatment plans of psychology are capable of helping new and seasoned clergy be competent and therefore effective in the area of pastoral counseling in general and pastoral diagnosis in particular.

15. The Significance of Pastoral Diagnosis

The phrase *pastoral diagnosis* in and of itself suggests an integration of two distinct but overlapping disciplines: religion and psychology. In his book *The Minister as Diagnostician*, Paul Pruyser describes the historical development of the term *diagnosis* as it concerns counseling by priests and pastors.[1] Broadly speaking, the term refers to the process by which authority figures in the church (i.e., pastors) identify, define, and analyze problems that concern the thoughts and resulting actions of their parishioners. A "pastoral diagnosis" is similar to a psychological or medical diagnosis inasmuch as the pastor is responsible for analyzing the symptoms of a problem (e.g., excessive drinking to the point that the personal and professional life of the individual is dysfunctional) and determining, through the use of his or her skills and resources, how the symptoms and the root problem may be effectively addressed through a pastoral counseling session. However, pastoral diagnosis is distinctly different from a psychological or medical diagnosis inasmuch as it necessarily uses the categories of theology, in conjunction with those of psychology, to explain and interpret human thought and behavior.

For example, a parishioner may drink excessively if she is coping with the emotional pain of having been physically abused as a child. However, the childhood abuse may also be interpreted by the parishioner as an indication that God does not love her. She may also believe that her "sinful" behavior as a young adult has somehow excluded her from the grace, forgiveness, and restoration of God. In other words, a psychological diagnosis of alcohol dependence must be addressed in conjunction with a pastoral diagnosis of "perceived alienation from God." The pastoral counselor is uniquely qualified to determine how the biblical message, as well as its interpretation in a particular context, is making the parishioner anxious, depressed, angry toward God, fearful of death and the afterlife, cynical about the power of God to intervene in human affairs, faithless, guilty to the point of immobilization or dysfunction, obsessed with the concept of shame, and dissociative (e.g., unconcerned with the business and events of this world). The pastoral counselor must also employ the categories of theology to address the parishioner's problems so that the parishioner can lead a healthy and productive spiritual, professional, and personal life.

The dimensions of the parishioner's life beyond matters of faith and belief are also to be addressed by the pastoral counselor. As a former inpatient and outpatient counselor, I understand the value of gathering data and qualitative information about the client through the intake process that far exceeds his or her belief system. Even though pastors are expected to be "resident experts" on matters of faith and theology, they may be more effective in addressing the parishioner's faith concerns if they have first understood and explored additional dimensions of that parishioner's life. Gaining a more holistic perspective on the parishioner's context will ground the process of assessing the parishioner's situation in order to help that person edit or reauthor his or her own personal narrative, preferably within a framework of faith.

What a person believes—about God, Scripture, the world, and self—may not always be beneficial to his or her overall functioning. This is as true in matters of Christian faith as it is in other aspects of life. For example, if a person believes that God is an unforgiving and unrelenting judge, that belief will influence the parishioner's ability to admit error, to forgive others or self, or to accept God's forgiveness. Therefore, it is essential to explore the parishioner's faith system along with additional clinical material so that a comprehensive picture of the postmodern parishioner can be presented in the case analysis. (See chapters 18 and 19.)

Of course, depending on the complexity and longevity of the parishioner's personal narrative, gaining a broader understanding of that context may require a longer-term counseling relationship, as opposed to the three to six sessions that are more typical of pastoral counseling.

16. Short-term Counseling, Long-term Relationships

Pastoral counseling is distinct from other forms of counseling inasmuch as sessions typically encompass one to six encounters, but the pastor-parishioner relationship may endure for the length of the parishioner's life. Psychological techniques used by pastoral counselors may assist the parishioner in helping to achieve goals (e.g., abstaining from alcohol), but the relationship between a pastor and parishioner may span the parishioner's entire life cycle.

As a doctoral student, I was responsible for presenting case studies of individuals who requested pastoral counseling. My fellow students and I were expected to learn the art and science of pastoral counseling by providing counseling to individuals for what was considered a significant period of time—a minimum of two sessions. While we had the option of meeting with our clients for the entire semester, generally speaking, the case studies that I presented during that process were indicative of short-term pastoral counseling.

Short-term pastoral counseling should not last more than one to two months or three to six weekly sessions. The nature and severity of the parishioner's presenting problem will help to determine the number of sessions.

For example, one parishioner may need pastoral counseling in the days immediately following the death of the loved one, but another may require grief counseling for the next couple of months, as well as the support of a comfort ministry or support group beyond that. One presenting problems (e.g., an interpersonal conflict between church members) may be resolved in one or two sessions; another problem (e.g., a crisis of faith) may take weeks to resolve. Ideally, the counseling pastor should plan to meet with the parishioner once a week for one to two months. If the parishioner needs considerable help beyond that period of time, the counselor should consider making a referral to a licensed mental health professional (e.g., psychologist or psychiatrist) who is sympathetic to the parishioner's religious or spiritual worldview.

The nature of the issues presented in a pastoral counseling session will be as varied as the people who seek counsel. Some parishioners will seek counseling as individuals; others will come as couples or families; still others will come individually because of an issue in their marriage or parenting relationships. The pastoral counselor should be prepared to address challenges that pertain to gender, race, culture, sexual orientation, and class, as well as conflict and crises that are associated with changes in the life cycle (e.g., birth and death, parenthood and retirement). Also, the counseling pastor should be prepared to address challenges that are specifically related to Christian faith, including those connected to a church's theological bent or doctrinal position. For example, a woman who has experienced the call to preach may feel anxious or angry because her denomination or local church will neither recognize nor ordain women as ministers. As another example, a parishioner may be wrestling with faith in a good and loving God when confronted with a particularly tragic or violent loss. In short, the pastoral counselor should approach the initial session as a *tabula rasa* (blank slate) so that he or she may be able to listen to the counselee and help determine the presenting problem.

The counseling relationship and its duration are also affected by parishioner progress and, unfortunately, parishioner relapse. Of course, the pastoral counselor's prayerful goal is to help parishioners demonstrate progress in their particular context. Indeed, the theme of the biblical narrative offers a promise that individuals can be "reborn" and "renewed" through the life-changing power of God. The gospel message gives hope to the hopeless and faith to the faithless, and that gospel message is a vital part of the pastoral counseling encounter. While that encounter is necessarily clinical in some aspects, it is also an arena where God is expected to show up and help the parishioner in some life-giving way. The pastoral counselor facilitates that by exemplifying the love of Christ throughout the therapeutic encounter, even if the parishioner's progress is minimal at best.

However long the tenure of the formal pastoral counseling sessions, the pastoral counselor never fully terminates his or her relationship with the parishioner. The two perhaps no longer meet formally or regularly, but the pastor will remain available and accessible as a listening ear, a prayerful support, and a confidential resource in times of renewed crisis or relapsed behavior, or just in the course of a life cycle when a person needs his or her shepherd.

17. Essential Elements of a Counseling Report

A counseling report contains clinical, medical, familial, cultural, social, and economic information about the client. In clinical contexts (e.g., hospitals, mental health treatment centers, therapy sessions) the process by which this information is gathered is called the "intake process." Pastoral counseling has appropriated and adapted this clinical process to generate a slightly less formal but still valuable overview of the new counseling client.

In her book *Diagnosis and Treatment Planning in Counseling*, Linda Seligman provides the structure of a comprehensive clinical report. Many of the questions that comprise this report will be beneficial to pastoral counselors who are attempting to understand parishioners beyond their theological belief system. In the clinical setting the intake interview initiates an admission process for an inpatient or outpatient program, and the interviewee and interviewer are usually strangers. In pastoral counseling the pastor often has a preexisting relationship with the parishioner, but it is still helpful to ask the intake-styled questions in the initial counseling session. The process will help the counseling pastor to see the parishioner in a new, more holistic light.

In clinical settings, the information gathered from the initial interview is generally organized according to the following categories: identifying information; presenting problem; present difficulties and previous disorders; present life situation; family; developmental history; medical history; mental status exam; diagnostic impression; treatment plan; and prognosis.[2] (For pastoral counseling purposes, I will elaborate on the most relevant of these categories in chapter 18.) Information concerning the religious belief system or rituals of the client may appear within many of these categories. Allow approximately one hour for the initial interview, which may be additional to the typical hour-long weekly session. However, the extra time and energy are essential to understand the parishioner from several different points of view, given that he or she has expressed an interest in receiving pastoral counseling over a significant period of time.

The Significance of Case Analysis

A case analysis examines and processes the information compiled in the counseling report. Whether done by the counseling pastor alone or in consultation with pastoral or clinical colleagues, this case analysis will include theological (faith-related) information as well as more traditional aspects of personal and medical history. The analysis offers the pastoral counselor a more holistic overview of the parishioner's situation and symptoms and empowers the counselor to approach the presenting problem in a more nuanced and holistic way.

For example, a couple seeking marriage counseling might reveal that one partner has a history of substance abuse or is currently unemployed. They might also disclose a struggle with infertility or challenges related to parenting. Each and every one of these circumstances will contribute a different kind of personal or relational stress that an effective counselor will want to address. Moreover, a thorough counseling report and case analysis may identify issues that demand longer-term or specialized counseling, to the benefit of both pastor and parishioner (not to mention others affected by the parishioner).

Ten Tips for the Initial Counseling Session

Most parishioners are familiar with their pastor as a congregational religious leader rather than as an individual pastoral counselor. Therefore, people who come to see a pastor for counseling may experience some degree of anxiety associated with providing a member of the clergy with detailed information about their psychological or medical history. The process of gathering this information may also prove awkward for clergy who are accustomed to interacting with parishioners primarily in corporate worship or small-group settings. Handle with extreme care the process of gathering information from parishioners, who often hold their pastor in high regard and deep affection.

A. Plan an initial informational session. During this session discuss the pastor's role as counselor and the scriptural basis that undergirds the process of pastoral counseling.

B. Establish the proposed length and frequency of the session. Will the sessions be thirty or sixty minutes long? Weekly or more or less often? At what point will progress be assessed?

C. Provide assurance that the counseling sessions are confidential, unless the parishioner has a plan to harm self or others. For example, in most states the abuse of children must be reported by the pastor to the appropriate authorities.

D. Share a copy of the counseling report form and explain the relevance of the questions. For example, a parishioner may wonder why the pastoral counselor needs to know about prescription medications. Explain how taking medications (or failing to take them) can influence symptoms, pastoral diagnosis, and progress.

E. Assure the parishioner that all written information will be kept under lock and key. However, some aspect of this information will be explored in each session in order to assess progress and evaluate status.

F. Make clear that the parishioner may discontinue counseling at any time. Especially within the context of parish ministry, assure the parishioner that the bond between pastor and parishioner will remain intact even if counseling is discontinued.

G. Be transparent about any fees and payment schedule, if payment is required for the pastoral counseling services. (This is more common outside of the parish setting.)

H. Discuss the implications and consequences associated with missing scheduled sessions. Repeated cancellations by the parishioner are often indicative of resistance to counseling.

I. Maintain healthy physical and emotional boundaries. In the pastoral counseling context it is usually best to limit physical contact to an initial professional handshake. (See chapter 5 for more about physical boundaries in particular.)

J. Listen to all the concerns or questions posed by the parishioner. Counseling sessions are primarily a time to listen and offer suggests in brief, not a time to preach.

18. Informational Categories for the Initial Interview

While each of the areas described below is considered a separate diagnostic category, their content may overlap as the parishioner's personal narrative unfolds. For example, the demographic data will inevitably connect with details related during exploration of the parishioner's current living situation, the family information will overlap with aspects of the developmental history, and so on. The pastoral counselor should be prepared for interplay between two or more of the diagnostic categories.

A. *Identifying information.* This encompasses demographic data, including age, sex, race or nationality, marital status, educational level, occupation, and place of residence. Questions about race and nationality might include clarification of native language (if English is not the first language) and religion (if the individual is not a member of the counselor's own church). In addition to asking about marital status and residential address, the counselor should inquire about cohabitants in the residence—dependent children, aging parents, extended family members, friends, or significant others. This data should also include the name and contact information of any agency or person who may have referred the individual for pastoral counseling.

Related to such demographic information is the indirect data that a pastoral counselor may glean from observation. How might the parishioner's physical appearance be described? How is he or she dressed, in terms of neatness, modesty, and appropriateness for the weather and setting? How does the parishioner present him or herself, and what kind of emotions are evident (i.e., "description of affect," in Seligman's terms)? Does the counselor detect any visible eccentricities or patterns of behavior? How can the individual's overall interaction with the counselor be described?

B. *Presenting problem.* Ask the parishioner about the primary reason for his or her visit. Inasmuch as the parishioner has requested pastoral counseling, the presenting problem may concern some aspect of religion or theology. It may concern the parishioner's perception of God's intervention (or lack thereof) in human affairs. However, do not assume that all parishioners want to talk about religion in general or the attributes of God in particular. Allow each parishioner to state the nature of the problem from his or her point of view. Some people will omit any mention of God in that initial session, and that is fine. The pastoral counselor can explore the faith-based connections in later sessions as seems appropriate or as prompted by the parishioner. For some Christians, their presenting problem may have no noticeable impact on their faith commitment and view of God. For others, they may be angry with God or feel otherwise reluctant to discuss matters of faith at first. Again, allow each individual to introduce the presenting problem in terms of his or her own choosing and allow the theological connections to emerge over time.

C. *Present difficulties and previous disorders.* During the initial session, listen carefully in an effort to determine how the parishioner's presenting problem is affecting other aspects of his or her life. For example, John may seek counseling because he cannot find a way to stop drinking. The pastoral counselor may ask questions such as these: How has drinking negatively affected your personal, professional, or spiritual life? How long have you been drinking? How often do you drink, and how much do you consume daily (or weekly)? Have you even been diagnosed with alcohol dependence by a medical or mental health professional? Have you ever been admitted to a detoxification unit, halfway house, or other transitional care facility?

Such questions are designed to encourage the parishioner to talk about his history and to explore the present effects of his drinking. The counselor who learns that John has been drinking heavily for two months may be prepared to approach the problem differently than the same counselor might approach Susan, who has been drinking for more than two decades. Certainly, that counselor may expect different responses from two people with such different histories.

D. *Present life situation.* In the initial interview, explore the parishioner's current life circumstance in broad and encompassing strokes. Not every aspect of a person's life will be in crisis, but insights into family, career, and social context may shed light on who that person is and what resources might be available to support him or her in a crisis.

Ask questions that will glean information pertaining to relationships with family and friends, as well as the stability and status of those relationships. Find out about the parishioner's current living situation beyond the demographic data of a physical address and fellow residents. Is it a safe environment? Is the person well rooted or highly mobile, a homeowner or renter, with a long commute or a convenient one? Ask about the parishioner's current occupational activities and whether those activities are full time or part time, salaried or volunteer. If the individual is a student, what is the nature of the program and what is its duration and stress level?

Life is about play as well as work, so inquire about social and leisure activities. How does the individual spend time outside of job, school, or family commitments? What activities and relationships are sources of satisfaction, support, and strength? Which are sources of stress, for better or worse? Ask about the parishioner's typical day and make note of details that cause agitation or amusement, frustration or fulfillment.

E. *Family.* If the pastoral counselor is attempting to follow these categories in order, some questions about the parishioner's family will have already been answered. Explore the relationships further with a series of questions about immediate and extended family members. These might include the following: Have you ever been married before? Do you have any children who do not live with you? Do you have any dependents who are not biologically related to you? How many members of your immediate family members currently live with you? The answers to such questions will assist in developing a comprehensive picture of the parishioner.

In many instances, of course, the parishioner's presenting problem is rooted in the stressed, strained, or conflict-laden relationships with particular family members. For example, Susan's two-decade-old alcoholism may be rooted in her shame about not being a "good" mother. John's more recent plunge into excessive drinking might be connected to the breakup of his marriage. George may be struggling with addiction to prescription medications after the death of his beloved spouse, and Charlene may be depressed in the midst of her mother's descent into dementia.

At other times, the presenting problem is connected to a parishioner's family of origin. Parishioners may require time to reveal childhood abuse or recognize the negative effects of more subtle dysfunctions, so do not expect to uncover an entire family history in the initial session. Use patience and care when attempting to get a parishioner to talk about family matters. Such openness is usually contingent upon developing and maintaining trust between counselor and parishioner.

F. *Developmental history.* Ask a series of questions regarding the developmental history of the parishioner. For example, inquire about the parishioner's birth history, early childhood, school years, and young adulthood. Past tragedies or traumas, particularly during the formative years between birth and age twenty-one, have a far-reaching impact on a person and may be partly or wholly responsible for the presenting problem of a parishioner. For example, was she abandoned as an infant? Did he witness abuse in his home? Did she spend any time in foster care? Did he come to this country as a refugee or as an undocumented immigrant? Was she a victim of date rape? Did he lose a parent to accident, disease, violence, or "merely" divorce? Is she a survivor of childhood cancer? Did he grow up with a special-needs sibling? Shocking or painful events that occur within the developmental cycle of the parishioner may be directly related to his or her relationship with immediate or extended family members.

G. *Medical and clinical history.* Because the pastoral counseling relationship is governed by ethics comparable to those that protect doctor-patient confidentiality, it is appropriate and even necessary to ask questions regarding the parishioner's medical or clinical history. Medical questions may include the following: Have you even been or are you currently under the care of a doctor? Have you been admitted to the hospital for a significant period of time? Have you ever been diagnosed with a chronic, debilitating, or terminal condition? The parishioner's medical history may reveal something significant about the mood of the client. For example, the parishioner who has been diagnosed with a terminal illness may be somewhat depressed or anxious to discuss issues regarding death and afterlife.

Similarly, exploration of the parishioner's clinical (mental health) history may also be insightful. Awareness that a parishioner has been diagnosed with antisocial personality disorder will significantly inform the pastoral counselor's interactions with a belligerent parishioner. Similarly, the counselor may be more understanding of an arrogant parishioner if that person acknowledges a previous diagnosis of a delusional disorder of the grandiose type.

The characteristics of these disorders, which are explained in the *Diagnostic and Statistical Manual of Mental Disorders IV* (DSM-IV), will help the pastoral counselor to understand certain aspects of the parishioner's personality. I recommend that all pastoral counselors purchase a copy of the DSM-IV, as well as the DSM-IV casebook. The DSM-IV will not explain how the parishioner became antisocial or delusional; however, it may suggest what the parishioner is inclined to say, do, and think inside and outside of the counseling session. In order to lead a parishioner out of what may be a confusing and fearful inner world, the counselor must understand something about that world, without becoming lost in it. Using a resource such as the DSM-IV, the pastoral counselor is equipped to listen to that world, comprehend its perceptions, and explain how the reality of Jesus can change it.

H. *Treatment plan.* The last category comes into play toward the end of the counseling cycle. For pastoral counseling, that may be the fourth of five planned sessions. As the cycle turns toward completion, begin to develop a treatment plan in collaboration with the parishioner. Both pastoral counselor and parishioner should have a copy of the treatment plan, which is always put into writing. The treatment plan should feature a series of short-term and long-term goals for the client. To return to the example of John, a newly confessed alcoholic, a short-term goal would be to refrain from taking a drink today—a goal that is renewed each day. A long-term goal may be to secure a sponsor and attend Alcoholics Anonymous meetings a minimum of three times each week for the next three months.

Encourage the parishioner to schedule a follow-up appointment with the pastoral counselor at the milestone designated by the long-term goal. For John, this would be after three months. For a different parishioner whose long-term goal is nearer at hand, the follow-up session might be just six to eight weeks later; for another, it might be further out, more along the lines of six months, depending on the nature of the presenting problem and of the goal. At that follow-up appointment the pastoral counselor will attempt to determine whether the parishioner is meeting the prescribed goals. If the parishioner has not had success thus far, the treatment plan may need to be revised, or the counselor may recommend additional resources (a support group, rehabilitation, referral to specialist) to meet the goal.

19. Understanding the Parishioner's Religious History

Having reviewed each of Seligman's diagnostic categories, the pastoral counselor may observe a noticeable omission: religious history. As a religious leader and person of faith, the counseling pastor will want to add questions to the initial interview, questions such as these: In which religious tradition(s) (if any) were you raised? How do you identify yourself in relation to religious faith (e.g., atheist, agnostic, lapsed Catholic, secular Jew, born-again Christian, mainline Protestant)? How new are you to your current faith identity or affiliation? How would you describe your relationship with God?

Gaining an understanding of the parishioner's religious history, including a family faith lineage, can be invaluable to the pastoral counselor. Sometimes, issues of faith and belief form the basis of the presenting problem. For example, Charlotte may have recently accepted Jesus as Lord and Savior in the Baptist church, and so she may seek counseling related to baptismal preparation for herself and may have questions about how to explain believer's baptism to her extended family, who are devout Catholics. In contrast, Louis may be a lifelong Pentecostal who has questions about the doctrine of predestination after joining a Reformed Church in his new community. Or perhaps the presenting problem involves premarital counseling for a couple whose marriage will join a woman who has been a Methodist since birth and a man who is new to the Christian faith altogether.

In all these situations, and many others, the pastoral counselor will benefit from having a good grasp of the parishioner's faith history and current theological position. This is all the more critical when the pastoral counselor is working with a couple or family group in which the members are a mix of ecumenical traditions, religious faiths, or disbelief in all things religious. For example, the agnostic individual who agrees to marriage counseling with an evangelical spouse may find it difficult to embrace the biblical principles or faith-based perspective offered by the pastoral counselor. In such scenarios the counselor must work to establish common ground upon which the pastor and parishioner(s) can agree. This might be an affirmation of the marriage vows, a recognition of the universal "golden rule," or a basic biblical principle that rings true regardless of one's faith position. Identifying that common ground will provide a firm foundation upon which the pastoral counselor and parishioner can develop or nurture a sense of trust.

Sometimes the religious history of a parishioner may unearth a kind of theological pathology—an erroneous, harmful, or delusional belief about God, about Scripture, or about self that is expressed in religious terms. For example, if Bill is convinced that "the devil made me do it," then he is unlikely to accept responsibility for his hot temper and anger management issues that have resulted in domestic violence and the destruction of his family. If Susan is excessively angry with God, blaming divine providence for a gene that predetermines her to be an alcoholic, she probably is not interested in AA's system of accountability. If Julie is skeptical about God's willingness to forgive, she may resist a healing process that leads her toward forgiving herself for getting pregnant as a teen and freeing her to grieve the loss of a baby given up for adoption.

More dramatic and problematic yet is the parishioner who believes that he is the manifestation of Jesus' second coming, or the person whose schizophrenia takes the form of demonic voices that tell her to harm herself or abuse others. All too often, mental health disorders find expression in religious thought and actions. A partial listing of these disorders is mentioned in the *Dictionary of Pastoral Care and Counseling*.[3]

20. Preparation Facilitates Relationship

Throughout this section I have provided theory and tasks associated with conducting the initial pastoral counseling session with the parishioner. These tasks have more to do with the functional, as opposed to the relational, aspects of pastoral counseling. It is important to note that the manner in which the pastoral counselor gathers information and explains the process of pastoral counseling will facilitate or hinder subsequent pastoral counseling sessions. The tools used to gather information should never obstruct or interfere with the pastoral counselor's overall care and concern for the parishioner.

Ask questions with empathy, and remember that the person who has a problem may be unwilling or unable to answer all of the questions in the initial or subsequent sessions. Remember that the pastoral counselor should not approach the initial interview in the manner of a researcher mining data on the Internet or in the special collections unit of a library. Instead of asking a barrage of successive questions, consider obtaining the information more organically, by having a conversation with the parishioner.

In short, the pastoral counselor must make painstaking effort to remember that the counselee is a child of

God with a need, as opposed to a walking problem that is to be interrogated through an initial session. The "interrogation method" of attaining information is common in mental health facilities where a counselor sees eight to ten clients in one day. The volume of clients and the insistence on third-party billing can cause these counselors to become emotionally detached from the clients. In contrast, the pastoral counselor should never become desensitized or emotionally detached from the parishioner. The initial counseling session should enhance the relationship between counselor and counselee by demonstrating the love of God and compassion of Christ by every word and gesture of the caring pastoral counselor.

Notes

1. Paul W. Pruyser, *The Minister as Diagnostician: Personal Problems in Pastoral Perspective* (Philadelphia: Westminster Press, 1976), 32–40.

2. Linda Seligman, *Diagnosis and Treatment Planning in Counseling* (New York: Human Sciences Press, 1986), 118–25.

3. Rodney J. Hunter, ed., *Dictionary of Pastoral Care and Counseling* (Nashville: Abingdon Press, 1990).

Pastoral Counseling with Couples

21. Individual or Group Counseling

In a clinical setting the majority of people who seek counseling do so as individuals. However, in the parish setting one may find a higher percentage of couples and families seeking pastoral counseling. In many cases pastoral counseling with couples is related to marriage, either preparing for it or responding to crises within the marital relationship. And in some cases it may become clear that an individual who is seeking counseling would benefit from at least a few sessions with his or her spouse, significant other, or family member(s).

I could list a wide variety of reasons for the greater incidence of individual counseling. To begin with, individual counseling is the form most recognized by insurance companies and mandated by courts, whereas premarital, marital, and family counseling typically is voluntary. Sometimes individual counseling is preferred by the parishioner. A young woman who feels ashamed of her eating disorder may be unwilling to discuss the matter with a parent present. An older man who is experiencing sexual dysfunction may find it impossible to talk candidly in front of his wife. A child who is asking difficult questions about faith is probably going to feel inhibited if mom or dad is also in the room. And finally, the societal preference for individual counseling may also be the product of a postmodern culture that emphasizes individuality and the right to both privacy and self-expression.

It is also true that couple or group counseling presents a variety of challenges. The voluntary nature of family and marriage counseling is a significant obstacle if the other spouse or family members are unwilling to participate in counseling sessions. Other times group counseling is hindered by the reality of conflicting schedules and the demands of job and family life. And as noted already, the participation of others in the counseling relationship may inhibit candid expression or feel like an intrusion on privacy. One parishioner, assuming "This is about me—it's my time to talk and process my own stuff," may resist sharing the counseling session with a spouse who will expect equal time and expression. Conversely, another parishioner might be afraid to discuss in the presence of his teenage children the behaviors that contribute to a family dysfunction: "This is private stuff. They don't need to be involved in my problems."

Of course, many of these reasons for preferring individual counseling are entirely legitimate. So, how does a pastoral counselor decide whether counseling should be one-on-one with a parishioner or involve others? Typically, this is determined by the nature of the presenting problem and the manner in which the initial request for counseling is expressed. Often, the decision to transition from individual sessions to couple or family counseling (or vice versa) will be made in conversation with the individual or other parties.

As you might expect (and perhaps have already experienced), a group counseling session presents very different dynamics than one-on-one counseling. This section explores some of the models and techniques that I have found to be effective in providing counseling with couples, and that may be adapted for use with family groups.

Even among couples the pastoral counselor may find it necessary to adjust or revise the models and strategies presented here. In the twenty-first century the diversity and the complexity of couple relationships are unprecedented. The pastoral counselor will still encounter the so-called traditional couples—the twenty-something, never-married, no-children, fresh-out-of-school man and woman seeking premarital counseling—as well as the married couple facing the transitions of midlife, which may include infidelity, cooling sexual desire, vocational transition, and the empty nest. Other couple configurations are hardly new to this generation: the cohabitating couple who now want to explore marriage (and who may or may not have children from their own or previous relationships); the older couple in which one or both individuals may be divorced or widowed; the couple who are creating a blended family with "stepchildren" and ex-spouses or former lovers with whom to negotiate; the thirty-, forty-, or fifty-something couple in which each partner has been living independently for a decade or more but must now consider how to integrate mature adult identities into the mystery of covenant marriage. Still other couples may seek pastoral counseling around issues that are increasingly prevalent (or at least more openly acknowledged) in this culture, issues that will challenge the new and the seasoned pastoral counselor alike.

The circumstances, personalities, and presenting problems in twenty-first-century relationships will vary widely. One thing remains: parishioners who are considering marriage, already married, or simply concerned about the functioning of their family are in need of pastoral counseling in every generation. This section is meant to be a resource for today's pastoral counselors who are attempting to meet that need in this time and place. Toward that goal, let us begin with some basic building blocks of couples counseling.

22. Putting the Reluctant Parishioner at Ease

The first task in any counseling encounter is to put the parishioner at ease, to lay a solid foundation of trust by establishing a comfortable and confidential environment for exploring deeply personal and often painful issues. That task is all the more critical in couples counseling because, in nearly every instance, one of the partners in that couple is earnest and eager to get started, while the other is visibly reluctant or even resistant to a greater or lesser degree.

In some cases the pastoral counselor will be familiar with the couple's issues and have a prior relationship with the eager parishioner, often because that person has already confided in or even participated in individual counseling with the pastor. Even if both members of the couple are new to the counseling relationship, however, the pastoral counselor will probably be able to identify the "reluctant" partner. Expressive body language such as lack of eye contact, poor posture, or crossed arms provides reliable clues. So does a depressed mood, blunt affect (lack of emotional expression), or minimal response to direct questions. All of these communicate to the pastoral counselor that this individual really does not want to be present.

Especially in situations of infidelity or other guilt-inspiring offenses, the reluctant partner may be participating only because his or her significant other has made counseling a prerequisite for a continued relationship. Other times, the reluctant partner is naturally more reticent or reserved and genuinely uncomfortable with the idea of "airing dirty laundry" with a third party. This is all the more likely if one member of the couple is not a church member or generally distrusts church leaders.

Whatever the source of the reluctance, in counseling with couples I recommend postponing the usual intake questions (described in Part III) until a welcoming and nonthreatening environment has been established. Jumping right into questions about mental health or medical history will seem clinical and off-putting, especially to the more uncertain partner. Similarly, an initial bombardment with questions regarding each person's psychosocial or family history is unlikely to establish a sense of trust with the individual who did not initiate the request for counseling. Instead, the pastor might begin with a personal introduction, as well as a brief description of what the pastoral counseling relationship is meant to offer to both members of the couple. Then, request a synopsis of the presenting problem from the perspective of each party, and finally begin to ask the basic questions of the intake.

For the pastor who has a good rapport with one of the parishioners but is now counseling the couple, demonstrating that rapport and openly discussing the existing relationship may be helpful in putting the reluctant partner at ease. Open with a light-hearted anecdote about a previous ministry interaction with the initiating parishioner, something that illustrates a congenial but professional connection; this will suggest that an element of trust and goodwill has already been established. Hopefully, the reluctant parishioner will understand the tacit invitation to enter into the existing relationship as a full partner and participant.

Of course, if reluctance has its roots in defensiveness, guilt, and shame, that individual may retreat even further behind an assumption that, in regard to the other partner, the pastoral counselor is "already on your side." In such cases the pastoral counselor would be wiser to begin with a warm welcome and open invitation to the reluctant parishioner to relate his or her side of the story first.

Anecdotally, it is often the male partner who is most resistant to counseling, but there certainly are exceptions to that "rule." Nevertheless, many men somehow find a way to receive pastoral counseling with their significant other. After several years of providing pastoral counseling to couples, I have heard many men state that pastoral counseling has helped to improve their relationship with their significant other.[1]

Pastoral counseling with couples will not be successful unless both parishioners have faith, trust, and confidence in the role, expertise, and demonstrable competence of the pastoral counselor. The effective pastoral counselor will undoubtedly be aware of and appropriate a variety of techniques and insights from psychology as well as resources and values from theology to help the couple in treatment. Help and healing for parishioners necessarily occur through the process of transference, an unconscious process through which the couple identifies or bonds with the pastoral counselor. According to Glen Gabbard, "By definition, transference is a repetition. The feelings associated with a figure from the past are being repeated with the psychiatrist in the present situation."[2] If the pastoral counselor presents as an empathic, trustworthy, and competent professional, the couple may identify with these attributes on a subconscious level. Their unconscious identification with these attributes will assist the couple in the counseling process. If the empathy and trust extended by the pastoral counselor are rejected by the couple, it may be because a previous pastoral counselor, psychologist, or psychiatrist misunderstood, abused, or neglected the role of counselor.

In short, the couple's acceptance of or resistance to pastoral counseling is occurring through the transference on an unconscious level. The pastoral counselor may have to raise and address questions about the couple's resistance to pastoral counseling or previous experiences with pastoral counselors in order for the couple to have faith, trust, and confidence in his or her current role, expertise, and demonstrable competence. Ultimately, it is through the conscious and unconscious rapport (transference) between the couple and the pastoral counselor that true help and healing will occur.

23. Scope and Timeline of Pastoral Counseling with Couples

People confront relational challenges on a daily basis. Couples often seek counseling because their lives have become unmanageable, and they need help bridging the issues that divide them. Those issues may be "big," such as adultery, addiction, or abuse, or the issues may start "small" but evolve from the mundane to the mammoth in times of stress. For example, finances are a common source of stress for couples, encompassing challenges with budgeting, balancing the checkbook, prioritizing expenditures and investments, managing debt, and rehabilitating a credit rating. But when one partner is under pressure at work or caring for an aging parent or facing a spiritual crossroads, the added stress can transform the monthly squabbles over paying the bills into threats of hiring divorce attorneys.

Pastoral counseling with couples often occurs when one or both members of the couple are experiencing financial, emotional, psychological, or spiritual crisis. The crisis usually develops over a period of time, be it days, weeks, months, or even years, although it may also have its source in a traumatic event with far-reaching impact. For instance, a couple may seem to weather the loss of a child with a spirit of unity, courage, and faith, but over time the lingering grief may erode the emotional, spiritual, or psychological health of one or both parents.

Because the presenting problem evolves over time, marriage counseling may be an exception to the general three-to-six-week time frame for short-term pastoral counseling. Counselor and couple alike may know that there is a problem (hopefully, one of the parishioners is not in denial); however, all three parties may not understand the genesis of the problem or why the problem persists in negatively affecting the couple's relationship. I strongly recommend that pastoral counseling with couples occur weekly over a period of five to fifteen weeks. This period of time enables the pastoral counselor to begin to develop a holistic picture of both individuals as well as the historic development of the presenting problem.

Longer-term counseling such as this demands that a pastoral counselor be intentional and strategic about the therapeutic process. By week six or eight, both the counselor and the couple need to feel that progress is being made. I recommend using the tool of a workbook specifically designed to help Christian couples address relational issues. Such workbooks typically are organized into ten to fifteen chapters, with each chapter exploring a specific topic and providing the couple with case studies and discussion questions tailored to a Christian audience.

The pastoral counselor may want to have several options on hand to offer the different couples who come seeking counseling. Some are intended for use in premarital counseling; others are written with the already married couple in mind. However, do not assume that a married couple cannot benefit from the fundamentals outlined in a book designed for engaged couples. Two people may be lawfully wedded for decades, but that does not necessarily mean that they have enjoyed (or even been exposed to) a loving, meaningful, and functional marriage.

One of the privileges of pastoral counseling, especially with couples, is the opportunity that it affords pastors to teach as well as to counsel. The answer to most relational problems is found in relearning ways of relating to one's partner. Facilitate the learning process by creating an environment that helps couples to avoid the characteristic "finger-pointing." A well-organized, biblically grounded, psychologically undergirded workbook can be an invaluable tool in that effort. And the "homework" common in such workbooks creates a record of progress over time for the couple and the counselor alike.

24. The Basics of Premarital Counseling

In my experience, couples who seek premarital counseling often are young adults, ranging in age from mid-twenties to mid-thirties, with the majority falling at the younger end of that range. These couples are predominantly heterosexual, and their request for pastoral counseling is almost always initiated by the woman. (In some instances I have even had couples seek counseling because they get a discount toward

the purchase of the marriage license if they receive premarital counseling! I appreciate the transparency of
such couples who candidly acknowledge the economic incentive to seek counseling. Especially among
younger couples, weddings are planned on a shoe-
string budget, so any financial savings are welcome.)
Because such counseling is deemed part of the clergy
job description, pastors in the parish setting often are
able to offer their premarital counseling services for no
fee, which is an additional blessing to the cash-
strapped couple.

I encourage all pastoral counselors to offer premarital counseling at no or low cost, especially for those
couples who seek it voluntarily. Not only can good
premarital counseling equip a newly married couple
to navigate the universal challenges of sharing a life
and home, but also it can avert relational catastrophes
if both partners remember and honor the strategies for
healthy communication, mutual respect, and covenant
love. Furthermore, for the pastoral counselor, premarital counseling is typically more rewarding, less
intense, and shorter term than marital or postmarital
(divorce) counseling. While marriage and postmarital
counseling often require five to fifteen weeks, premarital counseling is typically accomplished in just three
to six sessions.

Expectations and Assumptions

Numerous case studies in psychology demonstrate on empirical grounds a direct correlation between the client's motivation to succeed in counseling and his or her success in achieving goals in counseling. Couples seeking premarital counseling want to get married. They are present to discuss potential challenges and explore useful strategies for achieving a common goal: successful marriage. The engaged couple's newfound love and eager anticipation of their forthcoming wedding contributes to an amicable, if not celebratory, atmosphere within the premarital counseling session. This is in stark contrast with the married couple who seek a pastoral counselor only after a serious problem has occurred.

Of course, many couples (or individual partners) approach premarital counseling as a mere formality. They do not expect to discover anything earth-shattering or doubt-inspiring about their beloved. In the loving haze of betrothal, the primary goal of the sessions (a blissful marriage) is presumed to be a forgone conclusion. In such cases the pastoral counselor may find that one or both partners are disinterested in learning anything substantial or significant about their true love, and they certainly do not want to discover anything that might derail their well-advanced and often costly wedding plans. In the minds of such couples, pastoral counseling is, at most, expected to swiftly hammer out any late-developing issues that may eventually pose a threat to the marriage. Thus, the pastoral counselor is neither expected nor encouraged to lead them along a line of reasoning and self-examination that may lead to an obvious, albeit dreaded, conclusion: this couple should not get married. Whether the couple truly is a match made in heaven or instead is in love-blind denial, what should a pastoral counselor do when confronted with the assumption that she or he will endorse the couple's goal to get married?

The pastoral counselor has an ethical responsibility in two areas related to premarital counseling. First, provide the couple with competent and constructive pastoral counseling over the course of several weeks. That means making the sessions a priority and requiring the couple to do the same. (Some parish pastors make a minimum number of premarital counseling sessions a condition of agreeing to officiate the wedding ceremony or allowing use of the church facility.) It also means honoring the time allotted with an intentional process, and not allowing conversations to veer off into stories of romance or irrelevant tangents.

Second, affirm, challenge, and critically analyze each partner's belief system, as individuals and as a couple.

The belief system includes not only religious faith but also beliefs about marriage itself, gender roles, finances, family planning, parenting, in-law involvement, and the like. The pastoral counselor's goal is to help the couple explore their responses to a variety of different scenarios and to help them identify ways to cope with a variety of unprecedented emotional, psychological, spiritual, and financial challenges. Part of the ethical responsibility in premarital counseling is to create a learning environment that equips the couple with tools and resources to identify, confront, and avoid threats to the stability of their marriage.

It is not enough for the pastoral counselor to be an authority on matters pertaining to the biblical canon. Demonstrate flexibility and competence in a host of "extracanonical" subjects that will affect the material and spiritual lives of the couple as well. Affirm the institution of marriage, but challenge each partner's conception of it. Engage in a tug-of-war of Christian ideals with the couple, but avoid a dreaded win-lose scenario in which the counselor or the couple becomes the final authority of the meaning and significance of a Christian marriage.

The pastoral counselor has an ethical responsibility to fulfill the spirit of the couple's expectation, but also to lead them beyond. In a sense, premarital counseling requires the counselor to be both friend (supporter and encourager) and enemy (questioner and critic)—what today's young adults commonly call a "frenemy." Look forward to any opportunity to affirm and celebrate with a couple who want to embrace the long-standing institution of marriage within the Christian tradition. And do not be afraid to introduce your own expectations of the encounter in a firm and intentional way.

Topics and Strategies

As discussed in chapter 23 in connection with general couples counseling, pastoral counselors will find it helpful to use a workbook with engaged couples. Such a book usually provides a number of different case studies to read and respond to the issues in discussion or reflection questions. This kind of tool assists the counselor in defining the parameters of a healthy and functional marriage, and it facilitates discussion with couples around common challenges in the marriage relationship. Topics may include the following:

(1) *Money management*, from budgets and joint bank accounts to credit scores and debt consolidation, from investment strategies to spending priorities. An appalling number of marriages have crumbled under mundane and monstrous financial stresses.

(2) *Children and parenting*, from decisions about when to start (or stop) having kids to agreeing on disciplinary strategies, from identifying child care to dealing with infertility. Whether a couple begins with one or more children or never intend to become parents at all, the issue of children is another major source of marital conflict and rupture.

(3) *In-laws*, from the politics of navigating a spouse's family to decisions about caring for impoverished, ailing, or aging parents to balancing equal time among grandparents. In a sense, you do marry your spouse's entire family, for better or worse, and premarital counseling can help establish an early understanding between a couple about boundaries and responsibilities.

(4) *Career*, from questions of job relocation to continuing education, from issues of family leave to vocational transitions. In the twenty-first century, when both partners are typically employed when they come to the altar, married life will almost inevitably bring difficult decisions about balancing career with finances, parenting, and extended family relationships.

(5) *Home ownership*, from questions of renting versus buying, to decisions about where and when to purchase and about how much and how long the mortgage should be. Making the decision to buy (or not

buy) a home is a big and often contentious transition for couples.

(6) *Conflict,* from everyday debates about household chores to life-altering arguments about any of the issues named above. Related to the issue of conflict in marriage is the more basic matter of *communication*— styles, patterns, and effectiveness.

(7) *Faith,* from its centrality in the relationship to the specifics of its practice, from beliefs about key relational issues to decisions of childrearing within a particular tradition. Issues of faith and religious practice are particularly critical in interfaith marriages or between partners whose traditions or levels of commitment differ.

Of course, these are all universal and inevitable issues that eventually affect every marriage. The pastoral counselor may uncover more specific and specialized issues that require more attention and exploration—issues that may not be covered in a premarital workbook. Issues of addiction (substances, gambling, workaholism) or abuse (past or present) as well as other relational baggage such as divorce or children from previous relationships will add to the complexity and duration of premarital counseling.

Even if the couple considering marriage has engaged in a substantive discussion of some or all of the aforementioned issues, the ever-changing economic, political, and cultural landscape will affect the context in which these decisions were initially made. Premarital counseling offers an opportunity to reevaluate past decisions, and to establish strategies and tools for assessing and revisiting those decisions in the future. For example, a couple may plan to wait five years prior to having children. However, an unexpected pregnancy will likely affect their vocational and economic goals. The pastoral counselor can use case studies and questions to help the couple consider their present condition as well as future plans in light of a social and economic environment that is in constant flux.

How a couple responds to the case studies and related questions may reveal vast differences with regard to value systems and decision-making structures. Faced with such contrasting ideas about life and relationship, a couple may recognize the potential for schism in the future of their marriage. The pastoral counselor is then called to assist the couple in their present relationship, by identifying and acknowledging the competing interests or agendas and helping them reestablish common ground. In the end, the couple may choose to suspend judgment or to agree to disagree about a particular issue. That is acceptable, assuming that the pastoral counseling process has equipped them to (1) accept that they fundamentally disagree on that issue, and (2) identify ways in which they can enjoy a healthy and happy marriage in spite of their disagreement.

Those two decisions are vital to a successful marriage, and so leading a couple to affirm those decisions is the mark of effective premarital counseling. Consider that the major difference between premarital counseling and marriage or postmarital counseling is often just these two points. Couples who affirm them in premarital counseling choose to get married anyway, and they are more firmly established toward making that marriage last. In contrast, for couples who come to recognize a fundamental disagreement only long after the wedding, the question in counseling becomes "Can I embrace point two?" In other words, couples who emerge intact from effective premarital counseling emerge with a resolution to marry despite their obvious differences, and they have a plan for making it work. Unfortunately, couples who confront their fundamental differences only after the wedding vows have been spoken often find themselves questioning whether they can, at that late date, formulate a strategy for bridging the schism that they did not see coming.

The task of the pastor in couples counseling is comparable whether the counseling is premarital, marital, or postmarital. All couples are in need of the presence and guidance of the Holy Spirit, our comforter. The pastoral counselor has the privilege of reminding all couples about the presence and power of God as revealed through the Holy Spirit.

25. Identifying the Problems of the Married Couple

The content of counseling sessions with married couples is strikingly similar to the content of premarital pastoral counseling. Typically, both engaged and married couples are interested in discussing challenges related to finances, children, education, or vocation. However, providing pastoral counseling to married couples is different in two significant ways.

First, married couples seek pastoral counseling because of a clear and unmistakable presenting problem. (In contrast, premarital counseling is usually viewed as a preventive measure.) While most couples will have a variety of challenges throughout their relationship, the spouses seeking counseling will identify one problem that they cannot resolve on their own. The presence of that problem threatens the stability and longevity of their marriage.

Second, because of the presenting problem and frustration surrounding their inability to resolve it, one or both partners will express anger, confusion, bitterness, depression, loss of faith, or defensiveness. The couple has come to you as pastoral counselor because they are expecting a miracle from God through you.

To say the least, pastoral counseling with married couples is often an intense and exhausting but also spiritually gratifying experience. The following paragraphs highlight strategies to aid in addressing these challenges.

Seeing Life through Their Eyes

Couples in a troubled marriage often experience the world as chaotic, confused, and painful. A pastoral counselor becomes a companion on their journey through that world, and learning to see life through their eyes can be a difficult and draining process. In technical terms, the benefit of this process is called *empathy*, but the subconscious process in and of itself is called *transference*. The latter word describes how a parishioner's negative (or positive) emotions can transfer themselves to the counselor, and the word *counter-transference* describes the dynamic whereby the counselor returns those emotions to the parishioner in a reactive way.

I once had a colleague who insisted on using me as a sounding board. He would come to my office and share his ideas or vent his frustrations. Because he was angry about many aspects of his professional and personal life, he would communicate that anger to me through his loud and aggressive speech and expressive body language until I also became angry. Then having transferred his anger and frustration to me, my colleague would walk away. Consciously or unconsciously, he seemed determined to "sound off" until I had experienced at least a portion his angry and chaotic inner world.

Pastoral counseling should seek some degree of rapport between the counselor and the parishioner. It is difficult if not impossible to assist the couple in navigating the fear and confusion of their inner world if the pastoral counselor is unwilling or unable to experience a portion of it. The emotional and spiritual connections that enable the pastoral counselor to experience the parishioners' existential and spiritual angst are the same connections that will eventually contribute to the couple's healing and growth. Human beings respond to expressions of empathy; they are reassured and empowered when others comprehend their pain. Moreover, experiencing a degree of that pain also empowers the counselor to understand the nature of the problem and to discern the needed resolution. Thus, some transference is inevitable and even desirable. The Bible encourages us, "Rejoice with those who rejoice, weep with those who weep" (Romans

12:15). Sharing such moments of intense emotion is part of being a community, and it is a powerful element of being the community of faith.

However, when transference goes beyond empathy to return anger with anger or depression with hopelessness, the pastoral counselor has fallen prey to countertransference in a problematic and potentially harmful way. Be aware of the risk and seek a balance between experiencing the inner world of the parishioners without being overwhelmed by their emotions.

Reframing the Problem to Understand the Issues

Suppose a couple seeks pastoral counseling, and both spouses name finances as the presenting problem. However, in the initial session, the husband describes the nature of the financial issue in terms of his wife's overspending, while she acknowledges her spending but describes her husband's increasing focus on working long hours ("keeping up with the Joneses") to the detriment of their relationship. An attentive pastoral counselor will discover in these conflicting descriptions a clash of values. The husband values financial security, career advancement, and commitment to previously established goals as key to their marriage. In contrast, the wife values quality time and relational intimacy over such pragmatic concerns.

In this example, the pastoral counselor may recognize an obvious conflict in values, and by learning to see the presenting problem through each spouse's eyes (his, a threat to security and trust; hers, a sense of neglect and rejection), the counselor should be able to restate the issues with clarity and empathy. "I understand why you feel the way you do" may be followed by "Money is definitely a big part of the problem, but the two of you seem to value different things. Let's talk about those values." From there, facilitate a discussion about the couple's competing values and agendas, assisting the couple in gaining new insight into the nature of their presenting problem.

This is not an opportunity for the counseling pastor to preach to the couple. Rather, it is a chance to lead them to a moment of self-discovery. When the couple recognizes that the pastor has understood the depth of the problem from cognitive, emotive, and spiritual angles, they will more likely be open to encouragement and suggestions. Even if the couple knows what to do, that does not mean that they will take those steps. By reframing not only the problem but also the proposed solution, the pastoral counselor enables the couple to embrace their moment of self-discovery and work toward specific goals that are established in the counseling session.

Establishing Measurable Goals

The pastoral counselor should have a conversation with the couple in order to assist them in the process of identifying and pursuing goals that are to be achieved during and after the pastoral counseling sessions. These goals should be discussed throughout the counseling session but formalized and enumerated during the last three or four sessions. For example, if the presenting problem faced by the couple concerns their unwillingness or inability to discuss the management of their finances, the couple would formally state that they intend to have weekly discussions about their finances alone and with a financial advisor. This goal should be written down on paper. Since the couple has one presenting problem (i.e., one primary reason for seeking counsel), I would recommend that the couple and pastoral counselor establish a maximum of two or three goals. It is important to note the following: (1) the pastoral counselor should help in working toward these goals; (2) the couple may consciously and visibly work toward the achievement of these goals; (3) the couple may not achieve these goals in keeping with the target timeline. In some way, shape, or form the couple may consult the pastoral counselor after the counseling cycle has concluded in order to receive further help and support throughout the duration of their relationship.

The couple and pastoral counselor should be able to measure their progress toward achieving these goals. For example, if the goals relate to improved communication and increased savings, then they should count the number of hours they have met on a weekly basis to discuss their finances, and they should be able to see a quantifiable increase in their finances. If qualitative as opposed to quantitative goals are established during the pastoral counseling sessions, the couple should be able to recognize improvements in the way that they relate to each other—fewer incidents with raised voices or shed tears perhaps, and more positive encounters with shared laughter or renewed affection. The pastoral counselor should also be able to explain how the resources of the Christian faith (e.g., prayer) will be essential in helping them to achieve and/or maintain their goal(s).

The manner in which the qualitative or quantitative goals are to be measured should also be discussed during the pastoral counseling session. The couple must know beyond a shadow of a doubt if and when they have reached their goal(s).

Notes

1. A good resource is Murray Scher et al., eds., *Handbook of Counseling and Psychotherapy with*

Men (Newbury Park, CA: Sage Publications, 1987).

2. Glen O. Gabbard, *Psychodynamic Psychiatry in Clinical Practice* (Washington, DC: American Psychiatric Press, 1994), 69.

Pastoral Counseling and the Family Unit

26. The Church as Family, Families in Church

When I received my first appointment to a church, I was very excited about my initial pastoral charge, and I wanted to do a good job for the bishop, the denomination, the church members, my family, and all the individuals who had helped prepare me for a new beginning in my spiritual journey. I had my brand-new preaching commentaries, my Bible, my clergy robe, my first sermon, and I was ready for Sunday morning.

The ministry went well for several months, until I ran into a snag in the music department. As pastor, I wanted a popular medley of praise songs to be played a particular way for a certain period of time, and the minister of music wanted the same medley to be played a different way for a shorter period of time. I explained to the minister of music what I wanted done, as well as my reasons for making a particular decision. In our one-on-one meetings he stated that he understood my position, and he verbally agreed to embrace my vision as it concerned the overall thrust of the music ministry. However, week after week, I noticed that he continued to play the medley of songs in the manner that he wanted to play them as opposed to the way the way in which we had agreed upon in our personnel meeting.

Eventually, he told other members of the choir about our disagreement, and they told other members in the church. Finally, I met with the choir, and we discussed the issue. To my surprise, I found myself entertaining questions and comments about the hymns and praise music at the trustee meeting, the steward board meeting, the youth meeting, and several other significant meetings. In order to address and prayerfully resolve the issue, I called a church-wide meeting to hear everyone's opinions and work toward a common Christian goal as it concerned the music ministry.

We resolved the issue as a church family, but the experience reminded me of two vital insights. First, the church as a whole functions (or dysfunctions) as a family, and second, that church family is made up not so much of individuals but of individual families. A pastor's success in parish ministry hinges upon the ability to comprehend that insight and to provide corporate ministry with and pastoral counseling to those families. This section concerns an understanding of the family unit within the church, as well as a summary of the insights that I have found to be effective in working with families.

Traditional and Nontraditional Families

Families within the church can be broadly categorized into two distinct groups: the traditional family and the nontraditional family. The so-called traditional family consists of a husband, wife, and child or children. The three (or more) parties within this nuclear family traditionally live in the same house. The ties that bind the traditional family are those of biology, marriage, and in some cases adoption. In recent decades this category has often been expanded to encompass an increasing number of single-parent households as well as families that are blended by remarriage.

In contrast with the nuclear family, the extended family encompasses grandparents, great-grandparents, aunts and uncles, nieces and nephews, and cousins. When some of these extended family members reside under the same roof as the nuclear family, the resulting unit might well be considered nontraditional by the standards of middle-class United States culture. Of course, in times past and in cultures newer to the United States, it has been entirely in keeping with tradition to have multiple generations sharing a home. But in an age where it is more common for aging parents to live in retirement communities or assisted living facilities and for newly single parents to continue maintaining an independent household, an extended family that chooses to consolidate residences may be deemed "nontraditional."

By its very nature, the nontraditional family is difficult to define. We might characterize it as any group of people who have defined themselves as family. Included here may be foster families, transracial or older-child adoptive families, same-sex partnerships (with or without children), multigenerational families (as suggested above), and families of refuge (in which an at-risk friend or distant relative is welcomed in residence). Another nontraditional family unit is one in which members of that unit are separated by custody arrangements, incarceration, job or educational demands, or other extenuating circumstances. For example, the foster care system creates two nontraditional family units: the foster family, where a child is welcomed in a temporary arrangement of care, and the fractured nuclear family that is unable to care adequately for the needs of that child.

The "nontraditional" family label may also characterize a youth gang whose members see themselves as family (e.g., the famous gang *Mi Familia*). When I was a student at Harvard Divinity School, several local pastors formed an organization called the Ten Point Coalition in order to provide pastoral care and counseling to members of street gangs in the Boston area. Perhaps no family is more in need of pastoral care and welcome in the church. Young people seek identity, security, and protection within a gang, often when the nuclear or extended family is dysfunctional, putting the youth at risk.

Whatever the specific composition of a nontraditional family, the distinctive characteristic about its members is that they see themselves collectively and love one another as family. Their collective identity establishes emotional, psychological, cultural, ethical, and spiritual bonds that equal or transcend those of the traditional nuclear and extended family.

Just as family units may be traditional or nontraditional, the church as a family may also consist of traditional and nontraditional members. Some will be traditional in the sense of being saved, sanctified, tithing members of the congregation. Others will be nontraditional inasmuch as they associate with the church through visiting occasionally, attending events, participating in outreach, or accepting the caring ministries of the church. Some will be extended family because they live in the neighborhood, have access to church grounds and facilities, and turn to the church for weddings, funerals, and pastoral counseling. As leader of the local body of Christ, the pastor has a responsibility to care for all of these family members, even as Jesus did when teaching the disciples to love their neighbors (even nontraditional ones such as the Samaritan in the parable in Luke 10). And that will include pastoral counseling.

The Pastoral Counselor's Role in Nontraditional Families

In order to provide effective care to nontraditional families, the pastoral counselor must recognize and embrace the inherent worth of that family unit. Keep in mind that the so-called traditional nuclear family was something almost completely unknown in biblical history. Nearly every forebear of faith originated from or gave rise to what we now consider a nontraditional family.

Moses was transculturally adopted by an Egyptian princess, but he was fostered by his biological mother. Abraham had sons by several different women, including the Egyptian slave Hagar, who eventually would be forced to raise Ishmael as a single mother. Leah and Rachel shared Jacob as their husband, and then they offered him their maidservants as concubines and surrogates. Their twelve sons (and one named daughter) became a complex case study in blended family dysfunction. Separated from his nuclear family for the purposes of religious education and vocation, Samuel was raised by Eli, a man of no biological connection at all. And scholars teach us that many of the prophets probably formed their own "families" in the form of prophetic schools comprised of disciples and scribes who recorded their teachings.

Just as nontraditional families played a critical role in the history of our faith, so nontraditional families also hold potential to transform our future as the people of God. The pastor as counselor has a hallowed privilege and sacred responsibility to minister to such families in their times of greatest need. In receiving such ministry, even those families who are not currently part of the church family may be significantly influenced by the church and by our commitment to share God's love.

As the economic gulf continues to grow between the affluent and the impoverished throughout our global community, many families experience unemployment and underemployment. As the global community shrinks and conditions in other parts of the world deteriorate, an increasing number of immigrant families seek asylum or prosperity in our nation. As society becomes simultaneously more connected and more fragmented by technology, personal relationships are evolving, sometimes suffering from superficiality and the frenetic pace of life. In all these postmodern challenges the pastoral counselor has the opportunity to represent God's love face to face through meaningful personal encounters and sustained dialogue about real issues.

If God's people neglect to extend pastoral care and counseling to all families, we risk compounding the dysfunctions that are so prevalent in relationships in the twenty-first century, which will ultimately have a negatively impact on the church, its members, and its mission. As the influence of individual identifiers such as class, race, gender, and sexual orientation becomes more pronounced in the political and economic landscape of the United States, family units that reflect these distinctives will also become more prominent in church families.

As leaders in the church family, pastors who recognize and celebrate the inherent value of these diverse and distinctive family units will discover the rich resources that those families have to offer in the life and mission of the church. The relationship between the pastor and these nontraditional families, especially as nurtured through pastoral counseling, will not only define the spiritual climate of the church, but also expand the church's mission to share the gospel and minister to all people.

27. When Families Turn to a Pastor for Counseling

Historically, families remained in a particular local church or denomination because of a long-standing history with that church, often going back multiple generations. In the twenty-first century and in our highly mobile society, such "historic" church loyalty is far less common. Instead, families generally choose a local church based on factors that vary, from geographic proximity to dynamic worship to biblical preaching to a strong ministry to children and youth (or to singles, seniors, the homeless, etc.).

A congregation might be intentional about evangelism and outreach efforts. The leadership may develop a strategy to reach a particular demographic. However, in the end, a church has little control over who chooses to sit in the pews each week. Churches are voluntary institutions. Congregants are free to come and go as they please. And if church attendance is voluntary, participation in pastoral counseling is even more so.

What pastor has ever planned a sermon series designed to produce a flurry of appointments on his or her counseling calendar? Occasionally, a pastor might sense a need that inspires an invitation. Those with a shepherd's heart will learn to recognize the sound of a parishioner in distress—in a particularly fervent thank-you for a well-timed sermon, in an unusually tight handclasp or hug, in a voice that trembles, or in the arms wrapped a bit too tightly around a waist or across a chest. In response to such subtle signs, the inner pastoral counselor may step to the fore and quietly offer a follow-up conversation.

Such encounters are most likely to happen with individuals. In contrast, pastors will rarely initiate pastoral counseling sessions with families. In most instances, one or more members of the family will seek advice and support from the pastor. And as with couple's counseling, the family will already be wrestling with a specific presenting problem that goes beyond their usual challenges and everyday conflicts.

The pastor and family should be clear. A request for pastoral counseling should not masquerade as an opportunity for pointing out the shortcomings of the pastor or for stressing the historical significance of the family in the life and legacy of the church. If the initial session introduces a presenting problem that is directed at the pastor, a board, committee, or ministry, or at another individual or family in the congregation, then the pastoral counselor is entirely justified in cutting short the session and offering the family an opportunity to reschedule—a meeting, not a counseling session—to discuss whatever conflict or issue is named.

Conversely, the pastoral counseling session is not a private arena for the pastor to promote his or her political, economic, or social agenda. As inappropriate as a "bully pulpit" is in worship, the "bully counseling session" is even more unethical. A family's confession of financial troubles is not license to preach about their failure to tithe or to call for a faith pledge to the new capital campaign. A son whose girlfriend is pregnant is not a platform for proclaiming a stance on abortion, and a daughter who is suicidal because she was "outed" at school is not an excuse to pontificate about the pros and cons of gays in the military.

Families who request pastoral counseling do so because the family unit is experiencing a crisis. These families are often emotionally vulnerable, spiritually weak or confused, and relationally fractured or disintegrating. They are in desperate need of restructuring and restoration, and they have enough respect and love for the pastor to put faith in his or her integrity and ability to help. Thus, the pastoral counselor has personal and professional responsibility to allow the heart of Jesus and the mind of God to guide the content of the counseling session.

The legal and ethical obligations of the pastoral counselor will be discussed in more detail in Part VI. Suffice to say here that counseling sessions, especially with a family, are a time for listening much and talking little. Only through listening to the individual and collective narratives of the family unit will the pastoral counselor be able to discern and address the presenting problem.

A former pastor and mentor in the ministry told me, "Love the people, and invest in the people." Spending time with families in crisis through pastoral counseling sessions is a sure way of making a profound investment in the lives of people within the congregation. When the counseling experience is a positive one, the pastor-parishioner relationship is further deepened and strengthened, and the spiritual investment is sure to yield fruit of stability and abundant life for the entire church family. The following section concerns concrete strategies for making that investment.

28. Assessing the Family Structure in a Genogram

Family systems are complex, and not merely because of the number of people involved. Asking each member of the family unit to share his or her perspective on the current challenge is a helpful way to begin the initial session; but even if all of the narratives point toward a single presenting problem (and such unanimity would be surprising), the situation is unlikely to be that simple. Pastoral counselors who work with families should never assume that they have identified the presenting problem in the family unit without conducting a formal assessment of the unit according to established clinical guidelines. The assessment tools provided by the field of psychology are invaluable in helping the pastoral counselor to understand and engage the multiple systems that affect the family unit.

In most therapeutic settings part of the intake process includes the construction of a diagram that is similar to a family tree. In clinical circles that diagram is called a "genogram" (literally, a drawing of generations). According to Monica McGoldrick and Randy Gerson, a "genogram is format for drawing a family tree that records information about family members and their relationships over at least three generations.

Genograms display information graphically in a way that provide a quick gestalt of complex family patterns and a rich source of hypotheses about how a clinical problem may be connected to the family context and the evolution of both problem and context over time."[1]

Genograms are particularly useful in understanding generational patterns of addiction, abuse, and other relational dysfunctions. When generational patterns are absent, this is also helpful in directing the counselor to focus on environmental factors such as economics, physical and mental health, and trauma. Thus, the genogram both answers questions about a client's family and raises new lines of inquiry. I have found the genogram to be one of the most effective tools in understanding people in general and their supportive or conflictual relationships with members of the family in particular.

Constructing a Genogram (in Brief)

A genogram is a more complex version of a family tree. Where a family tree usually indicates only generational connections of birth and marriage, the genogram may be used to indicate emotional relationships (e.g., loving, hateful, hostile, manipulative, abusive, indifferent, estranged) and key social links (e.g., teacher-student, boss-employee, doctor-patient, pastor-parishioner).

Moreover, it can track medical and personal histories related to genetic diseases or disorders as well as unusual births and deaths.

Essentially, a genogram is comprised of shapes, lines, and colors, each of which has a range of patterns that is assigned a meaning. A square is used to represent a male, and a circle is used to represent a female. If a male and female are married, the pastoral counselor connects the two symbols with a horizontal straight line. If the couple is not married, a dotted line is used.

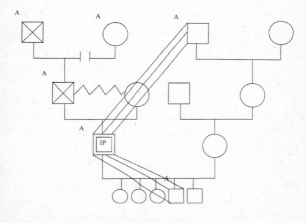

Sample Genogram

Spouses that are separated are connected with a straight line, but a single backslash is added. A double backslash indicates divorce. The diagram below illustrates these basic symbols and relationships. The client (also known as the IP, the "identified patient") is always denoted by a square within a square (male) or a circle within a circle (female).

Genograms are particularly valuable in working with families. For a family genogram, the parishioner who originally requested counseling is the IP. Pastoral counselors should attempt to construct a genogram that extends two generations back and (when possible) one or two generations forward—from grandparents to children or grandchildren—on both sides of the family, for both the IP and his or her spouse, if applicable. Note all births, deaths, marriages, divorces, and addictions on the genogram. If there are significant people outside of the household connected to the family, mark those persons and relationships as well. Finally, for each generational or interpersonal connection, note the following six types of relationships: very close or fused, fused and conflictual, poor or conflictual, close, estranged, or cutoff and distant.[2]

The sample genogram provided here represents a family unit engulfed in the cycle of addiction. Although the mother first suggested the idea of counseling, it was the father who ultimately requested pastoral counseling for his family because his son had been drinking alcohol and skipping school. Because the son was sixteen years old (thus, a minor), the genogram was constructed around the father (as IP), who also had a drinking problem. The genogram reveals a pattern of alcoholism in the family unit: the IP's father (now deceased) and grandparents were alcoholics. The genogram also reveals a very close relationship between the IP and his son, who is identified as an alcoholic. In contrast, the IP has a conflictual relationship with his spouse, and his deceased father had a conflictual relationship with his mother. The IP's grandparents were estranged. Notice that the genogram depicts a very close relationship between the IP and his spouse's grandfather, who is also an alcoholic.

What this sample genogram might suggest to the pastoral counselor is that the son's alcoholism and delinquency may be related to a pattern of alcoholism in his family. It also raises the possibility that his delinquency is connected to his parents' and grandparents' conflictual relationships. In the family counseling sessions, exploring issues in the parents' relationship may help address the son's desire to cope with reality through drinking. Addressing issues with regard to the father's (IP's) alcoholism (e.g., recommending a twelve-step program) may help the father and the son. Dealing with the fallout at school may require another pastoral function: the provision of a character reference so that the son can avoid expulsion.

McGoldrick and Gerson's *Genograms in Family Assessment* is an excellent resource for identifying the range and usage of symbols for pastoral counseling with families. Other resources and genogram tools are available online, varying in price from free to more than a thousand dollars, depending on the use required and the quality of the software. Detailed and expansive genograms, which address multiple generations, have the potential to provide the pastoral counselor with a wealth of information for family counseling sessions. Genograms may also be a teaching tool for family members who did not recognize the extent of the pathological behavior within the family system.

Lessons Learned from the Genogram

Genograms are valuable not only in educating parishioners in the counseling setting; they are also an essential tool for the pastoral counselor's self-education. I have worked with graduate and undergraduate students for several years now. When someone approaches me expressing an interest in professional ministry, I always make the case that every pastor needs a pastoral counselor. Then I invite them to engage in an exercise of self-analysis by constructing a personal genogram. Try creating one of your own.

This exercise of self-analysis will inevitably bring some unexpected (and often unwelcome) insight into your family history. Be willing to share the results of your genogram with a pastoral mentor or professional counselor or therapist. Patterns will emerge, and those patterns (e.g., divorce, depression, multiple marriages, suicide, teen pregnancy, estrangement) often require some hard emotional, psychological, and spiritual work. But it is good and necessary work. I constructed my first personal genogram as a doctoral student at Vanderbilt University, and I recall that the process was cathartic, informative, frightening, and exhausting.

The person seeking to become an effective pastoral counselor must have the emotional and mental fortitude to ask questions about his or her own immediate and extended family before venturing to ask questions about someone else. If we are unwilling to attempt a personal genogram, how will we deal with similar resistance from a parishioner? Even if the aspiring (or seasoned) pastoral counselor does not unearth any surprises, the exercise of using the genogram as an assessment tool will help that counselor make better use of it in counseling sessions.

29. Family Counseling over Time

Generally, a family unit seeks counseling when a crisis erupts and some members of the unit are attempting to cope with this crisis in ways that are socially unacceptable, professionally irresponsible, educationally detrimental, physically harmful, or completely illegal. In many cases the majority of family members have little to say during the session; instead, their intermittent responses often suggest that they ultimately are looking for an expedient solution to their problems. They are hoping for a quick fix—in the "guilty" individual(s), of course—so that life will return to normal.

The families that cannot move beyond that typically unrealistic expectation will not stick with the pastoral counseling. After two or three sessions, they will give up, or they will claim that everything is fine again. The challenge in family counseling is to get past the high emotion and (completely understandable) desire for an overnight cure and to gain the entire unit's commitment to doing the longer-term work. And family counseling usually is longer-term in nature, not only because of the complexity of the issues, but also because there are more voices in the room. Expect a minimum of five or six sessions to start, and be prepared to journey with them for a while beyond that, whether as a family unit or with selected individuals.

During the first session, begin by explaining that you want to hear from everyone, and that you need the others to listen respectfully until it is their turn to speak. Then invite each family member to share succinctly his or her own perspective on the problem. (You might go in age order, from oldest to youngest or vice versa, depending on the stated nature of the problem. Another option is to begin with the person who initiated the request for pastoral counseling or with the person who is identified as the biggest concern.) Hearing the narrative from all angles allows the pastoral counselor to construct a multidimensional understanding not only of the problem, but also of the family as a whole. Where do their perspectives conflict? Where do they converge? How do they react to one another in those places of conflict and convergence? What are the notable alliances and hostilities among specific family members?

During that initial session, expect people to cry, blame, yell, swear, avoid eye contact, and even walk out. But as firmly and compassionately as possible, remind all participants to refrain from interruption, and give each person equal time to share. The pastoral counselor's initial goal is to experience the family's world and to attempt to clarify and understand the unique perspectives of each person within that world. And as they share, be ready to make notes that will form the basis of a genogram, but do not attempt a methodical process for doing so. Just as a pastoral counselor will postpone the usual intake questions until a second session of marriage counseling, the counselor should merely observe and take informal notes in the first two or three sessions of family counseling. These notes can be used to begin genogram construction in between sessions, with a more intentional adding and filling in of details in session three or four, after a broader rapport is established and some of the crisis emotions have been processed.

Notes

1. Monica McGoldrick and Randy Gerson, *Genograms in Family Assessment* (New York: W. W. Norton, 1985), 1.

2. Ibid., 21.

*Practical Matters
in Pastoral Counseling*

30. Lawsuits in the Church

The apostle Paul writes, "For I do not do the good I want, but the evil I do not want is what I do. Now if I do what I do not want, it is no longer I that do it, but sin that dwells within me. So I find it to be a law that when I want to do what is good, evil lies close at hand" (Romans 7:19-21). He goes on to say, "Wretched man that I am! Who will rescue me from this body of death? Thanks be to God through Jesus Christ our Lord! So then, with my mind I am a slave to the law of God, but with my flesh I am a slave to the law of sin" (Romans 7:24-25).

People commit sinful acts. As fallible and imperfect creatures, we necessarily sin by thought, word, and deed. By God's grace, and through our confession and repentance, we are forgiven by God. The implications of certain types of sinful acts are clearly greater that the implications of others, however. For example, vastly different consequences will result when an adolescent tells a lie to avoid punishment at home versus when a witness lies under oath in court.

There are often legal implications of morally reprehensible or professionally unethical behaviors. This chapter will explore (1) the ways in which pastoral counselors have exposed themselves to liability; (2) strategies for avoiding exposure to liability; (3) the damage that can be done to the reputations (and financial standing) of the pastor, the local church, and the denomination once a lawsuit has been filed.

Ministry and the American Legal System, by Richard Couser, is an excellent primer for pastors and pastoral counselors who are seeking to provide counseling to parishioners. Couser's understanding of the historical and current relationship between the American legal system and the church far exceeds the discipline of pastoral care and counseling; therefore, I suggest that this text be a staple in the library of any pastor or pastoral counselor who is serious about Christian ministry.

According to Couser, lawsuits in the area of pastoral counseling are primarily centered on the following four areas: (1) defamation; (2) breach of privacy; (3) intentional infliction of emotional distress, sometimes called the tort of outrage or outrageous conduct; and (4) breach of fiduciary duty.[1] We will consider each one in turn as it may relate to pastoral counseling.

Defamation

"Defamation" refers to anything that may damage a person's reputation, diminishing the "esteem, respect, goodwill or confidence" that other people may hold that person in.[2] Inevitably it will encompass a fall from popular grace, or what in secular contexts is called "disgrace." In the pastoral counseling setting a charge of defamation may be avoided by refraining from any comment that disgraces or diminishes the character of the parishioner, whether face to face in the session or to others outside the session.

For example, people are sometimes a bit reluctant to receive advice from pastors. A parishioner who is uneasy with what is being said in the counseling session may lash out at the pastor. The pastoral counselor must always be a Christian as well as a professional; therefore, resist the urge to retaliate with a personal attack on the character of the person who has attacked you.

Alternatively, a pastor may become privy to personal information about a parishioner in a counseling session that may seem relevant in other settings. Refrain from alluding to such information in conversations with others; even if it were possible to honor the letter of confidentiality in terms of specifics, dropping hints about someone's personal issues may still defame his or her character and reputation in the church or community. In the next section I will discuss more about confidentiality in pastoral counseling.

Breach of Privacy

The phrase "breach of privacy" refers to the confidential nature of the pastoral counseling session. Without such assurance of confidentiality, few people would volunteer the personal details or permit such emotional vulnerability as a counseling session often requires. The parishioner must feel confident that the counselor will be trustworthy and ensure that "what happens in a counseling session stays in session."

Of course, the Bible covers this one fairly well with its prohibition on gossip. But the pastoral counselor has an additional ethical and professional responsibility not to disclose the content of the pastoral counseling session to anyone. Under defamation and breach of privacy laws, failure to keep confidentiality may have legal ramifications as well. There are just a few notable exceptions, some of which have legal demands attached:

■ A minor (child of eighteen years or under) is being harmed or about to be harmed.[3]

■ The parishioner expresses a plan to harm others.[4]

■ The parishioner expresses the intent to harm or kill himself or herself.[5]

■ The counselor has been ordered to do so by a court of law.

Concerning the last scenario, note that expectations of privileged privacy in a pastoral counseling session have changed. This is not only in the sense that attorney-client and physician-patient privileges have evolved, with many states limiting such privilege when a crime is involved. It is also in the sense of clergy-penitent privilege, or what is commonly associated with the Roman Catholic canon law that places a seal on the "sanctity of the confessional." Counseling pastors as well as pastoral counselors should become familiar with laws concerning privilege, privacy, and mandated reporting of child abuse in their state.

Tort of Outrage

This technical legal phrase is otherwise known as "intentional infliction of emotional distress." More simply, a tort is a civil wrong. In a pastoral counseling context this might be the product of "Bible bashing" or financial coercion. To avoid legal liability, pastors must be careful to apply church doctrine and discipline in such a way that parishioners are not pressured by the church to make personal and financial decisions that may not be in their best interest.

For example, there is the too-familiar story of the pastor who uses biblical proof texts and theological arguments to manipulate a parishioner into making a "sacrificial" financial gift, signing over her paycheck or the deed to his home. Such a gift produces financial hardship in that parishioner's life, which is interpreted legally as intentional infliction of emotional distress. Similarly, the counseling pastor who agrees to counsel a young man struggling with his sexual identity and who uses pastoral authority to induce greater shame and depression is guilty of the tort of outrage. Any time that a pastor or counselor attempts to coerce a parishioner into choosing to act or embracing a particular point of view, that pastoral counselor may be found guilty of the tort of outrage. Take care never to create or contribute to a scenario that causes an individual, couple, or family unit to experience financial or emotional distress.

Breach of Fiduciary Duty

The term *fiduciary* refers to trust that has been placed in someone or something else. Indeed, it is considered the highest standard of care in legal terms, wherein the fiduciary is expected to be loyal to his or her charge to the extent that everything done as fiduciary is for that person's benefit and well-being.

In the pastoral counseling context the parishioner entrusts him or herself—spiritually, emotionally, psychologically, even physically—to the counselor. The pastor is responsible to care for that parishioner in a trustworthy manner. Any of the three preceding legal liabilities mentioned thus far might also be considered a breach of fiduciary duty, at least in the ethical sense. For example, with God's help, the pastoral counselor is entrusted with the task of restoring, rehabilitating, and redeeming a parishioner's character. Defaming that person's character is a violation of that trust. Similarly, the counselor who inflicts emotional distress instead of offering healing words and compassion has violated the parishioner's trust.

In relation to legal liability, a breach of fiduciary trust is typically more quantifiable, such as misappropriating or embezzling funds for the fiduciary's own benefit. (This is why most churches have a system of checks and balances so that offerings are counted in the presence of at least one witness, and the pastor is rarely included in that group.) In pastoral counseling situations a breach of fiduciary duty may be related to a conflict of interests when counseling couples or families. For example, if a wife feels that the counseling pastor is favoring her husband to the detriment of her (or their) best interests, the pastor may become liable for breach of fiduciary duty. In general, the pastor should never misuse or forsake the client's trust in order to gain something politically, economically, socially, professionally, or financially. As the saying goes, for the pastoral counselor, "It isn't about you."

31. Credentials for Pastoral Counseling

A person does not necessarily need formal credentials to preach the gospel of Jesus Christ. Many people preach about the love of God and salvation through Jesus Christ without being recognized by a denomination or even a local church body. Yet, there are rights and privileges associated with formal credentials for ministry. A license to preach or the ordination to Christian ministry is typically granted after an individual has sought a particular level of education and demonstrated certain ministry gifts or a vocational calling to serve God's people. Such credentials are usually bestowed by a congregation or by the denominational hierarchy, and they come with rights and responsibilities, such as the privilege of officiating at weddings or at the Communion table and the expectation of abiding by a professional code of ethics.

In much the same way that any Christian may proclaim the gospel message (i.e., preach), so any member of the clergy may perform counseling services. Because such religious counseling is considered part of their professional (pastoral) duties, clergy generally are exempt from the various licensing requirements that govern mental health providers, from psychiatrists and psychologists to Christian counselors and therapists. But note: "Exemptions from licensing may be limited to ordained clergy however."[6]

Ronald Bullis and Cynthia Mazur explain that the religious counselor's exemptions from specialized licensure requirement rest on four factors. The counselor must be

■ ordained, licensed, or otherwise recognized by a national religious body (denomination);

■ supervised by his or her denominational judicatory;

■ engaging in counseling as an ordinary and regular part of his or her duties;

■ avoid using (or implying the use of) regulated professional titles (e.g., therapist, psychologist).[7]

Thus, in many parish settings the clergyperson who offers pastoral care in the form of pastoral counseling will not possess specialized credentials for that counseling beyond ordination to the Christian ministry itself. He or she may have had a seminary course or two in pastoral counseling, which provide fundamentals and an introduction to ethics and strategies. And in many church settings where pastoral counseling is limited to the short-term care of three to six weekly sessions, such training and education are functionally sufficient.

It is worth noting that some ministers feel a call to pastoral counseling as a specialized vocation. Such individuals may seek graduate- or postgraduate-level education in the field of pastoral counseling and then pursue licensing and endorsement from a national denomination or convention. (Such endorsement is comparable to that required of chaplains in the military, hospitals, and other settings.) For these ministry specialists, counseling is more likely to fall into the long-term category. The licensed pastoral counselor often may function as a member of a larger team of mental health professionals in order to deal with more complex issues. Moreover, with the vast majority of the licensed pastoral counselor's time spent in session with clients, his or her vulnerability to charges of malpractice make the purchase of malpractice insurance a necessity.

In fact, even those pastors who offer pastoral counseling under the "religious counselor exemption" should consider purchasing malpractice insurance. I strongly recommend it. We live in a litigious society, and unfortunately pastoral counselors and counseling pastors are not exempt from civil lawsuits filed by current or former counselees. The claims that are filed against a counselor may be a result of a real or perceived violation of the pastoral counselor's code of ethics (discussed in the next section below). Without the protection of malpractice insurance, a successful civil lawsuit could lead to a financially devastating experience (i.e., personal or congregational bankruptcy), not to mention the damage to the pastoral counselor's ministry and reputation. There are companies that specialize in providing professional liability or malpractice insurance to pastoral counselors. I strongly recommend that every pastoral counselor purchase malpractice insurance in order to help to address civil claims.

Identifying and Abiding by a Code of Ethics

Generally, the code of ethics for ministers is set for by a denomination's doctrine or discipline. Individuals seeking ordination may be required to sign a code of ethics document, which states rules of conduct for the minister as a member of the clergy. Research (or refresh your memory on) your own faith traditions code of ministerial ethics. (For an example, see appendix B.)

I also recommend that clergy who provide pastoral counseling primarily in parish settings become familiar with the code of ethics of the American Association of Pastoral Counselors (AAPC). The AAPC code of ethics addresses topics that include, but are not limited to, client relationships, confidentiality, sexual ethics, and integrity in advertising members' pastoral counseling services.

The pastoral counseling skills of new and seasoned clergy may also be enhanced though membership in the AAPC, whose members are those who support its mission "to bring healing, hope, and wholeness to individuals, families, and communities."[8]

32. Referrals in Pastoral Counseling

In a clinical setting referrals are made on a routine basis. When I worked in an inpatient and outpatient facility, we referred clients to various other facilities after they received treatment, since our mental health facility did not possess the human (personnel), capital (building space), financial, or medical resources to continue helping the clients. Our resources were inadequate for the task of providing holistic care for them.

In the field of pastoral counseling there are comparable concerns for identifying and adequately distributing resources for parishioners. Pastoral counselors are sometimes unable to provide the holistic care required by a parishioner; therefore, the pastor will make a referral. The referral process, at its best, finds its genesis in the pastoral counselor's determination to provide the best care possible for the parishioner. And a wise, self-aware, and humble counselor will recognize when that best care is best provided by someone else—someone with more time, more experience, or more education and expertise in a particular area. Ultimately, love, care, and concern for the parishioner are the motivating factors for making a referral.

Even though a parishioner may have contacted the pastor or pastoral counselor primarily for spiritual guidance regarding a particular problem or concern, it may become evident that the psychological, medical, or financial needs of the parishioner far exceed the resources of the pastoral counselor. The pastoral counselor should refer any parishioner whose presenting problem or related issues cannot be resolved through the short-term or general nature of counseling sessions in the parish setting. This is true for the parishioner suffering from schizophrenia or an obsessive need to self-mutilate. It is also true for the person who has been homeless or unemployed for an extended period of time. The former clients are best served by a clinical referral to a licensed mental health provider that can offer more holistic (psychiatric or medical) care. The latter will benefit from a social services referral to an organization that is better equipped to navigate the system and access benefits.

Even though a referral may mark the end of pastoral counseling sessions, it may also be appropriate for a pastoral counselor to continue meeting with the parishioner even after a successful referral. For example, a psychiatric referral will provide a parishioner with needed medication, such as antidepressants, but that parishioner may still desire and benefit from the spiritual counsel and prayerful support offered in pastoral counseling.

How to Refer

To some extent, the pastoral counselor must rely upon his or her ministerial experience, professional or clinical competence, and spiritual discernment in order to determine the appropriate timing for a referral. A basic rule to keep in mind, however, is that if a parishioner's issue (e.g., alcohol intoxication) is interfering with his or her ability to receive pastoral counseling, the pastor should make a referral immediately.

In a clinical setting referrals are usually initiated by the counselor or therapist after securing the client's written consent. Because most pastors and even many pastoral counselors are not qualified to make clinical diagnoses or equipped to deal with third-party insurances and so on, I do not recommend calling an inpatient or outpatient facility on behalf of a parishioner. (A notable exception, of course, is a medical emergency, such as a seizure or heart attack, during a pastoral counseling session.) Even in suggesting to the parishioner that a referral is in his or her best interests, the pastoral counselor should avoid using any technical, medical, or psychological language because of the legal and medical implications of conveying such information incorrectly.

I recommend a simple process for pastoral counselors making a referral. First, call the provider or facility (e.g., homeless shelter or rehab center) to obtain information about the services that they provide. Then, provide the pertinent information—name, contact information, brief description of the services or expertise—in writing to the parishioner. Encourage him or her to make the first contact, and do not hesitate to discreetly follow up later and find out how things are going (i.e., if contact was ever made). In this way, the pastoral counselor avoids any liability associated with conveying the details of the parishioner's complex and sensitive personal information to a third party. Moreover, there is the added benefit that the parishioner must take responsibility for his or her holistic recovery.

Where to Refer

Veteran pastors and counselors will soon compile a list of clinical facilities, social service agencies, and other specialists in their community. When in doubt, a pastor might call a ministerial colleague for suggestions if faced with a new issue. Also, if possible, the pastoral counselor should visit local facilities and become acquainted with the staff that will ultimately provide services to the parishioner. Even though the pastoral counselor is not housed at the facility (e.g., hospital or halfway house), he or she will become an integral part of the holistic team charged with the responsibility of providing the best possible care for the parishioner.

Parishioners usually are open to the idea of accepting a referral from the pastoral counseling and receiving helpful services from other people and institutions, far more so than individuals who are compelled to accept counseling by a court (e.g., court mandated for anger issues or DUI, or the state's prerequisite for regaining custody of a child) and show up just to mark time or get it over with. Remember that most people in pastoral counseling are there voluntarily; they genuinely want to receive help from the counselor, and that often includes whatever other source the pastor may recommend.

Many empirical studies have concluded that the client's motivation for change is an important factor in his or her ability to reach the stated goals in therapy. Pastoral counselors are fortunate to work with a constituency of persons who generally are motivated to change or improve their thoughts and behavior. I believe that parishioners' success in pastoral counseling (e.g., their ability to achieve goals and achieve insight with regard to the nature of their presenting problem) is rooted in the internal motivation to voluntarily seek the help of God and of the pastoral counselor to overcome challenges in their spiritual life.

Notes

1. Richard B. Couser, *Ministry and the American Legal System: A Guide for Clergy, Lay Workers, and Congregations* (Minneapolis: Fortress Press, 1993), 270.

2. Ibid.

3. Ibid, 268. Note that twenty-six states now include clergy among mandated reporters of child abuse. See www.childwelfare.gov/systemwide/laws_policies/statu tes/manda.cfm.

4. Ibid.

5. Ibid.

6. Ibid., 266.

7. Ronald K. Bullis and Cynthia S. Mazur, *Legal Issues and Religious Counseling* (Louisville: Westminster/John Knox Press, 1993), 48.

8. For membership standards and more information about AAPC, visit www.aapc.org.

Addiction Counseling

33. A Crash Course on Addiction

I have counseled chemical-dependent individuals in both inpatient and outpatient facilities. Even though I am no longer working in those clinical settings, my experience continues in my capacity as university chaplain and pastor. What I have discovered in those more recent experiences is that many people who seek pastoral counseling are willing to disclose and further explore past and present struggles with addiction. Pastoral counselors will find it helpful to look out for clues to such a history.

You might notice a parishioner wearing a chain with a pendant that says "NA." Ask if the initials signify "Narcotics Anonymous." An affirmative response may open the door to an in-depth discussion about his or her recovery. Another parishioner might admit to being in recovery during the course of describing his or her presenting problems, allowing the pastoral counselor to ask how the recovery process (or the original addiction) may be aiding or exacerbating that presenting problem. Some parishioners might make passing mention of attending "meetings"—a subtle clue that they include Alcoholics Anonymous (AA), Gamblers Anonymous (GA), or other twelve-step program meetings as part of their recovery process. Follow up by inquiring about the type of addiction (alcohol, prescription or illegal drugs, gambling) and the effectiveness of those meetings in supporting their recovery.

Of course, people who are engaged in a counseling process may not be acting on their addiction at that time. Some may be clean or sober for years; others may just be "currently sober" or be three days or three weeks clean. The latter are most vulnerable to relapse, particularly if they are attempting to beat their addiction alone, without engaging in a more holistic recovery process, such as that outlined by a twelve-step program. In some cases they have not hit "rock bottom," where the consequences of their addiction have finally outweighed the pleasure of indulging it. In those cases they probably have not learned any relapse prevention strategies.

What does it take to stay sober? The success stories feature extremely motivated individuals. If you ask them if they are consistently attending AA or NA meetings, they will respond yes. If you ask them if they have a sponsor, they will respond yes. If you ask them if they have a relationship with God or a Higher Power, they will respond yes.

Addictions cover a wide range of substances and behaviors, from alcohol to tobacco, from prescription medications to illegal drugs, from overeating to anorexia and bulimia, from gambling to cutting, to more "benign" addictive activities such as shopping or video games. However, because my experience is limited to drug and alcohol counseling, and because intervention with other types of addictions varies widely, this section is intended primarily for pastoral counselors who want to work with chemical-dependent parishioners, especially those individuals who have a sincere desire to achieve and maintain sobriety.

It is my prayer that all parishioners who are addicted to a mind- or mood-altering substance achieve sobriety. It is also my prayer that pastoral counselors working with these parishioners, who may be sober one Sunday and inebriated the next, continue to recognize that they are and will always be God's children. Jesus makes it perfectly clear that these members of the Christian community, as the meek and "poor in spirit" (Matthew 5:3), are still blessed by God.

When I first began working with people who are chemical-dependent, I saw them as addicts—beings completely and fundamentally different from myself. I noticed the needle tracks in their arms. I watched them stumbling into the detoxification unit, sometimes in handcuffs. I noticed their missing teeth, torn clothes, and battered faces, their paranoia, rage, and physical and mental exhaustion. Many of them had lost their jobs, and most resorted to the detox unit because their family members would not let them in the house until they were sober again.

However, as I began to look beyond their physical appearance and listen to their personal stories, I noticed that I had a number of things in common with these addicts. Most of us had graduated from high school; we all had parents and siblings, and many of us had spouses and children. At some point, we had held jobs, and most of us believed in God or a Higher Power. How had these human beings, who were so much like me, come to this place of dependence and self-destructive behavior? Why were they so preoccupied with a substance or habit that was unhealthy and (in many cases) illegal? Among drug addicts in particular the addiction leads to dealing what they use; among addicts of all types the self-destructive habits led to the implosion of relationships and careers and sometimes physical violence to self or others.

Cycle of Addiction

What pastoral counselors must come to understand is the complexity of the cycle of addiction and the process of recovery. It is an irrational cycle inasmuch as the addict believes that he or she can control the use of a substance or behavior, even though the addiction has been proven to create a life of professional and personal dysfunction. This cycle is complicated because addiction often has a biological or chemical component, in that the body physically craves the drug of choice.

In contrast, the process of recovery has a rational component as the addict learns relapse-prevention strategies so that he or she will be able to recognize and avoid people, places, or things that cause a mental relapse (thinking about renewed use), which usually proceeds to a physical relapse (actual use). And just as the cycle of addiction has a biological component, the recovery process often has a complementary medical component when a psychiatrist prescribes selected medications (e.g., methadone for heroin addicts) so that the client will not self-medicate.

Finally, the cycle of addiction requires a spiritual component in order to initiate a process of recovery by acknowledging that God or a Higher Power can help the addict to achieve and maintain recovery. This is a component where the pastoral counselor is well equipped to support and encourage the recovering addict through prayer, biblical principles, and discussion of faith matters.

Educate Yourself Any pastoral counselor who is earnestly attempting to provide adequate care to individuals with addictive personalities, and especially those who are dependent on chemical substances, needs to understand the basic facts about how the mind and body respond to an addiction as well as how the mind and body can effectively recover from one. A fundamental understanding of the biological, chemical, and neurological effects of addiction will also assist the pastoral counselor in meaningful conversations with healthcare professionals who are also committed to the parishioner's recovery.

Look for literature published by Alcoholics Anonymous, Narcotics Anonymous, Gamblers Anonymous, and Al-Anon that offers support to the families of alcoholics. Attend support groups that are open to individuals who are not addicts. Read and observe in order to learn everything you can about the addiction cycle and recovery process and their effects on various aspects of the addict's life and relationships. Finally, have conversations with mental health professionals as well as with individuals who know about the recovery process, because they have already achieved a significant amount of sober time.

Be Part of a Holistic Team Because addiction itself is so complex, providing effective treatment for people with addictions is also complex. No one person should attempt to do it alone. Factors such as the "drug" of choice (whether a literal substance or an addictive behavior), the frequency of behavior or quantity of use, the duration of an addiction (months, years, decades), the psychological and medical history of the patient (diagnoses additional to the addiction), and the stability and security of living arrangements and relationships (transience, lack of family support) may make recovery a daunting if not seemingly impossible task for a parishioner. Fortunately, a host of institutions are willing and able to provide various professional services to these parishioners. The pastoral counselor becomes a critical member of a holistic team to facilitate and support recovery and reintegration into mainstream life and restored relationships.

Healthcare providers. Doctors, nurses, and clinic workers address the biological and chemical components of the cycle. This is particularly vital when a diagnosis of an addictive personality is combined with a diagnosis of sexually transmitted disease (from infected needles or risky sexual contact), physical injury (from bad company or accidents under the influence), exposure (from sleeping on the streets), cancer or disease (from toxins in abused substances), and so on.

Mental health professionals. Just as regular healthcare providers address physical health, professionals in the field of mental health, including psychologists and psychiatrists, address psychoemotional health aspects of addiction and recovery. As noted above, a psychiatrist may prescribe approved medications to ease the trauma of withdrawal from a particularly harsh drug or to treat chemical imbalances related to schizophrenia and other mental illnesses. A psychologist may treat a person whose addiction is connected to depression, personality disorders, or past trauma.

Social workers. These public servants intervene when addiction deprives an addict of a living wage, adequate housing, and other practical needs. They are able to assist the person in need with navigating the governmental agencies and institutions in order to get the necessary help. Social workers will also get involved if an addict's behaviors put children, aging parents, or a spouse at risk.

Sponsors and support groups. When the first human being was created, the Creator looked at the man and said, "It is not good that the man should be alone" (Genesis 2:18). No one should have to walk through life's valleys or climb life's mountains alone. Support groups, such as AA, NA, and GA meetings, offer not only a community of encouragement and empathy but also the accountability and guidance of a sponsor—someone who has personally walked the journey called "recovery" and who can point out the stumbling blocks and milestones along the way. (When counseling couples or families where one or more person is struggling with addiction, the counselor should encourage other family members to attend Al-Anon meetings, where their needs may also be supported.)

Clergy and communities of faith. As an ordained member of the clergy, the pastoral counselor is competent to address spiritual and social components of the process. The community of faith can serve, in part, as another community of support, encouragement, and accountability, not only for the recovering addict but also for his or her family and friends.

Make the Appropriate Referrals In summary, while being an integral part of this holistic team, the wise pastor will be prepared to assemble quickly a trusted network of professionals to whom he or she can refer or connect the parishioner who is struggling with addiction, whether as the presenting problem or as a related issue. In many larger towns and cities a team of professionals who are willing to assist parishioners in the recovery process has already been established. It is understood that the parishioner reserves the right to refuse the holistic care offered through the pastoral counselor's referral. Be sure to obtain the individual's written consent before contacting anyone in a new or established support network.

The pastoral counselor who ministers in an area where such a network must be developed from the ground up should not hesitate to contact "secular" professionals. Even those whose specialties are firmly grounded in the empirical sciences are often interested in hearing the theological perspectives of the pastoral counselor when it concerns the holistic care of a patient or client. After all, Alcoholics Anonymous, which has had a tremendous success rate in helping people achieve sobriety, places strong emphasis on the individual's relationship with a Higher Power.

Take the time to meet with the professionals before you add them to your referral list. If possible, ask other clergy in your area who might have had interactions with the persons or agencies and get their feedback on the quality of care offered. And when meeting with the professionals, who in many cases have impressive degrees, an esoteric vocabulary, and significant financial resources, resist any inclination to be shy or intimidated. Be congenial, engaged, and caring. Convey to the team that both the pastor-parishioner relationship and the parishioner's relationship with God are significant resources in that client's recovery process. The presence of the pastor or pastoral counselor will remind the team that care is a holistic process, and that the parishioner's comprehensive treatment plan and full recovery are dependent on the team's ability to work effectively together.

34. Tough Questions, Rough Referrals

When a parishioner comes to request pastor counseling, it is incumbent on the pastor or pastoral counselor to ask a series of tough questions in conjunction with the basic initial interview. Answers to these questions should be kept confidential unless they fall within the legal criteria mentioned in chapter 30.

After beginning with the introductory questions of name and presenting problem, the pastoral counselor should ask these two questions: (1) Are you under the influence of alcohol or another drug right now? (2) Are you having any thoughts about injuring yourself or someone else?

Under the Influence

If a parishioner admits to being under the influence during a session, follow up with these questions:

■ What is your drug of choice (e.g., alcohol, prescription medications, illegal drugs)?

■ How much do you use and how often do you use?

■ How long have you being using?

■ What is the longest period of time you have been clean or sober?

Equipped with this information, the counselor takes the next step, which is to refer the chemical-addicted parishioner to an appropriate rehabilitation program. Be sure to explain that pastoral counseling will begin when he or she is in recovery (i.e., not currently under the influence of the substance or habit of choice).

Violent Thoughts or Intent

If a parishioner responds in the affirmative to having thoughts or plans to harm self or others, you will definitely need to make a referral. When confronted with a person who acknowledges a plan to harm or kill someone else (i.e., to commit assault or murder), termi-

nate the pastoral counseling session immediately, and
after the parishioner has left the facility, call the police.
Do not attempt to contact law enforcement with the
person in your presence.

If the person is planning suicide or self-harm, I do
not recommend abruptly terminating a counseling session with that person with a well-meaning suggestion
that he or she go to a local hospital. Instead, call the
local hospital immediately and either drive the parishioner to the emergency room or sit with him or her
until the ambulance arrives. The parishioner who is
planning self-harm needs to be under constant supervi-
sion by the pastoral counselor or paramedics until a
psychologist or psychiatrist can evaluate him or her.

I recommend calling the hospital because the
resources available to assist suicidal individuals vary
from city to city. However, the staff of the emergency
room at the local hospital will be able to identify immediately the mental health professionals within the hospital or throughout the city who are capable of effectively addressing this life-threatening emergency.

Questions about inebriation or violent intent may
seem to be a bit intrusive and judgmental in nature,
especially in the initial session. The pastor may be
reluctant to ask, and the parishioner is likely to resist
answering because the questions compel him or her to

confront the addiction. However, the answers will facilitate the honest and effective exchange between pastoral counselor and parishioner. This is particularly true if the parishioner does not perceive the addiction to be the (presenting) problem. For example, a parishioner may identify a concern with his or her spouse as the presenting problem, and so a dialogical exchange between the counselor and client may address the relationship between addiction and marriage.

Personal Faith

While the intake process will include questions about the parishioner's belief system, the counselor who is working with an acknowledged addict will find it helpful to ask one more key question: "Do you believe in God" (or what the Alcoholics Anonymous program calls "a power greater than ourselves")? The more a pastoral counselor can learn about the parishioner's faith at the outset of the session, the better equipped the counselor will be. Usually, parishioners have accepted the theological worldview of their pastors. However, the theological perspective of the addicted parishioner may be quite different from that of the pastor or pastoral counselor.

Addicts often blame God for their existential and spiritual predicament; therefore, traditional "God" language may not be helpful to them in their recovery. The attributes of their Higher Power may or may not be similar to the Christian concept of God. For example, they may affirm a Higher Power's omnipotence, but not its essential goodness. Therefore, the pastor should make painstaking effort to understand an individual's beliefs before assuming that an understanding of a Higher Power is beneficial in the recovery process.

35. The Power of Reframing a Personal Narrative

People with addictive personalities, even those who have acknowledged their addiction, are not helped by simplistic instructions such as "Stop doing drugs" or "Just say no." Telling them to stop is neither useful nor effective. In fact, trying to shame them or make them feel guilty for their addiction usually increases anxiety and exacerbates a preexisting sense of guilt, which in turn negatively impacts their recovery. Instead, the most important task of the pastoral counselor is to listen to, as opposed to preach at, the client.

Addictions are secondary problems that cloak a primary issue, one that may not be readily disclosed by the parishioner or identified by the pastoral counselor. Substance abuse and other addictive behaviors often provide people with a temporary escape from the things that torment them, psychologically or environmentally. Chemical dependency in particular represents an attempt to escape the images, individuals, or institutions that injure or intimidate on a daily basis. So, a pastoral counselor who is working with a recovering addict should listen closely to the client's personal narrative. Doing so will (1) unearth the mental images of emotionally painful experiences that are being masked by the addictive behaviors; (2) recognize the self-defeating messages a parishioner may be rehearsing; and (3) identify individuals and institutions that have a role in either aiding or inhibiting the parishioner's recovery. The images may then be reframed; the messages may be edited; relationships with individuals and institutions may be strengthened or severed.

For example, a young woman with a history of cutting herself may be punishing herself because of misplaced guilt after suffering sexual abuse. Certainly, this is a case for referral to a mental health professional. However, assuming that such a woman has entered recovery and is seeking relationship counseling, the pastoral counselor may continue the recovery process by helping her to reframe those images. By learning to shift the guilt and responsibility onto the perpetrator, the young woman may experience new freedom to love and be loved by a spouse whom she has persistently held at an emotional distance.

The recovering alcoholic may have been drinking to drown out memories of a father who repeatedly communicated, "You're a loser," or to fulfill the prophecy of a mother who declared, "Your daddy was a drunk, and you'll be just like him." The pastoral counselor can hold that client accountable for attending regular AA meetings and also offer family counseling to help repair relationships or identify family patterns of verbal abuse.

And the adolescent recovering from an addiction to prescription medications may have started popping pills because living with a clinically depressed (and equally addicted) mother proved to be contagious. In such a case, social services may have intervened to remove the teen from an at-risk home, and both mother and child may now be seeing a therapist who specializes in depression. The pastoral counselor may be able to support them in family counseling sessions by rebuilding trust in the family unit and establishing new patterns of communication and healthy interdependence.

In all such circumstances life has presented the parishioner with a personal history, the details of which are fixed. No one can rewind time and prevent the abuse, take back the harmful words, or eliminate whatever caused the caregiver's depression. And all should be referred to specialists to address their long-term recovery needs. However, the beliefs and values within the narrative (e.g., negative beliefs about one-self and God) may be edited with the help of the pastoral counselor.

When working with parishioners to assist in them in editing and reauthoring their personal narratives, the pastoral counselor uses the resources of Christian faith. For example, the Bible includes stories about people who experienced traumatic circumstances and dysfunctional family lives (e.g., the sibling rivalry and violence of Joseph and his brothers; the grief of Job and his wife; the incestuous rape and subsequent desolation of Tamar). These stories and their faith-based significance may be discussed with the client as a tool in editing and rewriting a personal narrative.

The pastoral counselor may also identify positive interpersonal and familial relationships, both in Scripture and in the church. Often, parishioners who are in recovery have never seen or been involved in healthy and functional relationships; therefore, they may have constructed a narrative that suggests that all relationships are unhealthy, abusive, and dysfunctional.

Another resource of Christian faith is the language of prayer. Prayer may inform or remind the parishioner that God loves humankind, and that God is at work in human affairs. This theological position may cause the parishioner to reexamine his or her notion of a dispassionate, irresponsive, and cruel God who is not interested in the well-being of human beings.

Assisting the parishioner in the process of reframing a personal narrative is a challenging process. But ultimately, we are all works in progress, editing and reframing our own narratives to the extent possible. Our lives are interconnected, and God's love for us all is what makes a "threefold cord" possible (see Ecclesiastes 4:12). It is through this sense of interconnection that we will, by God's grace, be able to reach our full human potential.

Bereavement Counseling

36. Understanding the Grieving Parishioner

Grief comes to all people, and each person responds to the experience in different ways. Like most pastors, I have visited the houses of people who were grieving. These visits have preceded and succeeded the funerals of the deceased. In every visit at least one family member had requested my presence; occasionally, however, other family members have viewed me as an intruder in their grief. In such situations the pastor has a responsibility to provide pastoral care to the family members who have requested his or her presence while simultaneously respecting the wishes of other family members, who may be in the same room, who may not want to participate in the pastoral counseling. Do not take such "rejection" personally; it may be a rejection of the reality of death itself. Anger displayed toward the pastor or pastoral counselor may be a reflection of anger directed at God for "taking" the life of a loved one.

When responding to the request to visit the home of grieving parishioners, recognize and respect your place and role within the entire grieving family unit. Even though a number of grieving individuals may be present, I recommend that you initially engage with those who have requested your pastoral presence. However, do not be hesitant about extending an invitation to all of the family members to receive pastoral counseling at some point in the future.

Bereavement counseling is one of the most common encounters in the pastoral context, whether it consists of formal therapeutic sessions over a period of three to six weeks or of the pastoral moment of a hospital or home visit in the immediate wake of a death. It can also be one of the most powerfully transforming and significant encounters between pastor and parishioner—an opportunity to bring a ministry of presence as well as word into the lives of the surviving family members and friends.

Most often, pastors will provide bereavement counseling for people who are grieving the loss of a close family member (e.g., child, spouse, parent). In these cases parishioners are seeking the comfort and advice of the pastoral counselor in the belief that the resources of the Christian faith are able to help them cope with their loss, be it from natural causes or from accident, illness, or violence.

Even though pastoral counseling primarily concerns the theoretical intersection of psychology, religion, and culture, the counseling pastor may be asked to assist the parishioner with the detailed scheduling and overall logistics of the funeral arrangements as they concern the deceased. The pastor may want to ask the parishioner a series of questions that provide guidance through practical details:

■ How will funeral costs be handled?

■ What is the name and contact information for the funeral company that will receive the body?

■ Who will participate in the funeral (e.g., minister, eulogist, family, friends, dignitaries)?

■ What will be the date, time, and location of the funeral (or memorial) service?

If possible, questions regarding the practical logistics of the funeral arrangements should be addressed at the outset of the initial counseling session. The majority of the time in counseling session(s) should be spent addressing the anxiety of the parishioner and the specific set of circumstances that are related to the process of grief.

It is worth noting, however, that death is not the only circumstance that requires a kind of bereavement counseling. Although they may not frame their presenting problem as grief, parishioners may be bereaved as a result of a loss of job or marriage, a failed adoption, or a broken engagement. A significant portion of the initial pastoral counseling should be spent helping to clarify the presenting problem of the parishioner (e.g., the specific person, issue, or circumstance that initiated the grieving process) so that the pastor can employ specific techniques in aiding the parishioner in coping with a loss.

Understanding the Uniqueness of Grief

A number of factors influence the unique nature of personal grief, and the pastoral counselor will want to listen carefully and ask gently probing questions to discern the complexities of each unique situation. Consider the following aspects of grief.

Relationship with the Deceased. Were the bereaved par-ishioners connected to the deceased by biology, marriage, or adoption, or by a less formal bond? What degree of intimacy did they share, emotionally, physically, psychologically? Was their relationship close or distant, hostile or loving, short-term or long-term?

What relational issues may complicate the survivor's ability to grieve the loss and be reconciled to life without the deceased? For example, if the deceased was an ex-husband who was abusive or adulterous, grief may be mingled with anger, guilt, shame, or resentment. Contrast that with the grief of a woman who has just lost her devoted spouse of fifty-four years.

Circumstances of Death. People tend to grieve rather differently for the death of the ninety-year-old grandparent who has lived a full life and passed peacefully in sleep than for the sixteen-year-old star athlete who is killed in a skiing accident. Similarly, the parents of a stillborn infant will grieve differently than the new father whose wife succumbs to postpartum depression and commits suicide. The age and health of the deceased as well as the nature of the death—its cause, timing, or expectation—influence significantly the nature of the survivors' grief.

Age and Experience of the Survivor. Children grieve differently than teens, who grieve differently than adults, based largely on their developmental stage in life and the coping skills that they have accrued. That is not to say that adults will handle grief better than children. People who reach adulthood without ever suffering the death of someone close may find themselves utterly at a loss to deal with the experience of grief. They might be contrasted with children in the foster care system, who experience so many losses at a young age that death may seem to have little impact at all. And those children whose responses are blunted by repeated traumas are in contrast with the octogenarian who has come to view the deaths of peers with composure, recognizing that it comes with age.

Existing Support Systems. The support systems available to the bereaved parishioner may include family members, friends, other church members, a specific comfort ministry of the church, or a specific group (e.g., Mothers Against Drunk Driving). The primary goal of such support systems is to shepherd survivors through the cycle of grief. The pastoral counselor is responsible not only for being part of that support network but also for assessing the strength of the existing supports, as well as the need for additional resources. Become familiar with a support resource prior to recommending it to the survivor. For example, the pastoral counselor should know the fees (if any) charged by a resource organization or individual, the particular theological or philosophical bent of the organization, and the length of time a survivor is expected to engage with the resource. As appropriate, the pastor may also help the grief-stricken parishioner by making initial contact with an individual or organization to request support.

Other Complicating Stressors. A wide variety of psychosocial stressors may contribute to or obstruct a survivor's grief journey. Some stressors are pragmatic, such as concerns about finances, employment, housing, education, or care of dependent children or aging parents. Some stressors are relational, such as when there is strife among surviving family members or when a death occurs in the midst of a survivor's own divorce or custody battle. Other stressors may be clinical, related to preexisting conditions in mental or physical health. Pastoral counseling sessions offer the opportunity to explore anxieties, fears, or symptoms that point to additional stressors. Here is another area where the pastoral counselor may want to refer the parishioner to others who are equipped to address the external stressor.

View of Death. Death is sometimes an intellectually confusing, psychologically disorienting, emotionally painful, and intensely traumatic experience for the parishioner. Knowing what a bereaved parishioner knows about the Christian faith and believes about death will better equip the pastoral counselor to respond to that person's grief. The pastoral counseling moment represents an interplay between listening and affirming. The pastor, regardless of his or her personal beliefs, has an ethical and professional obligation to listen to the parishioner's own view of death, including any unique, unorthodox, or even "pagan" perspectives about the afterlife (e.g., reincarnation, purgatory, nirvana, no afterlife at all). At the same time, the parishioner has sought pastoral counseling from a member of the Christian clergy, and so the pastor may be expected to affirm Christian teachings about death, resurrection, and eternal life in God's presence. However, do not use the counseling moment to ridicule, berate, chastise, or preach to the parishioner. A gentle affirmation of Christian faith will have more of an impact than a scathing critique of the parishioner's convictions.

Sources of Comfort

In addition to seeking pastoral counseling, most people find comfort in talking with family and friends, participating in a support group, writing in a journal, and participating in rituals of remembrance such as visiting the gravesite, sprinkling ashes, or hosting a memorial service. In time, the grief subsides into an occasional sadness or fleeting moments of pain. The process may take months adding up to a year or more, but it does run its course.

For other people, however, the socially acceptable ways of processing grief do not adequately address the emotional pain of loss. They may withdraw from other relationships or show signs of clinical depression. Others get stuck in a pattern of aggression or hostility to protect their own sense of vulnerability. Some will turn to alcohol and illegal drugs to help numb the pain; some become increasingly dependent on medications (e.g., antidepressants, sleep aids) initially prescribed to deal with the first ravages of grief.

In many such cases these individuals will seek counseling to deal with other presenting problems, never realizing that those problems derive from the emotional pain of unresolved grief. The pastoral counselor who unearths such hidden grief has the privilege of helping such parishioners to acknowledge the loss and learn to deal with that pain in more healthy and coherent ways.

37. Understanding the Cycle of Grief

People respond to grief events differently. In order to minister effectively to a person, couple, or family that is grieving, the pastoral counselor should understand that grieving is a process that has phases or stages: shock, denial, acceptance, anger, despair, and reengagement in life.

Stages of Grief

These phases do not occur in a particular sequence, and it is common for a grieving individual to revisit one or more of the stages during the process. One person may experience anger prior to experiencing acceptance or despair before anger about a loved one's death; another may swing between two or more stages, with anger vying with despair in a cycle of emotional pain. In whatever sequence the stages occur or recur, and however long a particular stage may last, it is the pastoral counselor's responsibility to (1) understand the phases of the cycle; (2) know where parishioners are within the cycle; and (3) shepherd people through the various phases so that they that the do not become fixated or "stuck" in a particular phase.

Shock. During the initial phase of shock a parishioner cannot comprehend what has happened. The death of a loved one is often beyond our ability to comprehend and respond to; therefore, we react. When told the news of someone's death, a person may cry out, collapse in a chair or on the floor, clutch at another person or nearby object, or merely stare blankly in lack of understanding. This shock may last only a moment or two, particularly if the death is expected and the family has gathered to share the final hours. It may also last for hours or days, which is more common with a sudden, violent, or premature death.

When possible, the presence of the pastoral counselor during this stage is an important opportunity to offer not words, but rather the ministry of a quiet, listening presence. The pastoral counselor may express condolences simply and then sit quietly with the parishioner. Some people will not want to talk; do not force it. Others will talk incessantly, and their words may or may not be coherent. Whether in silence or in a flood of words, the pastor can attend closely to the bereaved individual. Those early moments of grief may offer valuable insights into the life of the deceased or into the heart and mind of the surviving loved one.

In some cases grief may devastate a person so completely that the assistance of a trained medical professional is needed. This may manifest itself in inconsolable hysterics or in prolonged, blank unresponsiveness. In those situations contact the trauma center at the local hospital and convey information regarding the behavior of the parishioner.

Denial. In the phase of denial bereaved individuals refuse to believe what has happened. They may suggest that someone has made an error with regard to the pronunciation of the death. Some may become angry and accuse the doctor or police officer or whoever has delivered the news of death of lying. Others may staunchly refuse to believe that the sudden death of the person is within the realm of possibility.

The pastoral counselor should not attempt to "force" the parishioner out of this stage of denial by repetition of the news or by providing "proof" of the loved one's death. All human beings have defense mechanisms, and denial is a subconscious coping mechanism that prevents some people from having a complete mental breakdown. Because it is a function of the subconscious mind, if a person is truly in denial, he or she will not recognize that fact. Just remember that denial is usually a temporary phase in the grief process. Eventually, the parishioner will come to terms with what has happened. Until then, the pastoral counselor may embody the ministry of presence, following the example of Jesus, who became "God with us" to demonstrate the immanent nature of God.

Acceptance. In the acceptance stage the person has moved past incomprehension (shock) and refusal (denial) to understanding. Intellectually, he or she has accepted the facts about what has happened: a loved one has died. Even though the stage acceptance is a rational act, it is still a psychologically and emotionally painful act. In fact, acceptance may permit the bereaved individual the first real opportunity to deal with the emotions of grief and loss. The parishioner may display a range of responses, from questioning or disagreeing with "God's decision" to call the loved one home, to analyzing the circumstances which led the person's death, to beginning to blame self, others, and even the deceased for whatever set of circumstances led to the person's death.

The process by which the parishioner has truly come to terms with what has happened may provide the pastoral counselor with the first opportunity to have a substantive and coherent conversation with the parishioner regarding his or her feelings and, as appropriate, the circumstances surrounding the loved one's death. As in the other stages, the pastoral counselor should allow the parishioner to determine content, direction, and tempo of the conversational exchange. The pastoral counselor may want to use the resources of the faith (e.g., prayer and Scripture) to affirm the parishioner.

Anger. Yes, the parishioner has accepted on a cerebral, intellectual level that the death is a reality. However, bitter anger may remain about the death of the loved one. This anger may be directed at the deceased person, and this is especially common after a suicide or death that is connected with poor choices on the part of the lost loved one. Survivors may be angry with the medical professionals who could not save the loved one, or the person whose actions (or lack of action) contributed to the death. They may also be bitterly angry with themselves for a real or perceived role in causing (or not preventing) the death. Of course, they may also direct a strong dose of anger toward God for allowing the tragic event to occur.

The pastoral counselor should recognize that anger is a stage in the cycle of grief. He or she should allow the parishioner to express anger in the pastoral counseling session; however, the pastoral counselor should never tolerate being verbally or physically abused by the parishioner (see more on this below). If the parishioner has expressed anger toward the counselor, it is important to remember not to take this personally. In reality, the parishioner is angry at the set of circumstances surrounding the events. The wise pastoral counselor will listen without reacting to the anger, refraining from a response that tries to compete in volume or intensity but instead answering with a quiet murmur of compassion or gentle question to explore the pain behind the anger. The pastoral counselor's willingness and ability to listen to the parishioner's anger is an essential factor in the process of helping the parishioner to resolve that anger.

The pastoral counselor should not seek to dismiss or minimize the parishioner's anger. The pastoral counselor should also refrain from encouraging it. The pastoral counselor should recognize that anger represents a fundamental and psychologically necessary stage (for some people) in the grieving process. It is important to note, however, that the pastoral counselor should resist being verbally assaulted or abused by the angry and possibly enraged parishioner. The pastoral counselor may need to cancel the counseling session or excuse himself or herself from the home of the parishioner if the parishioner is unable to express anger in an appropriate and socially acceptable manner.

Despair. All too often, after blaming the victim, others, themselves, or God for the death of their loved one, parishioners enter into a depression. In that state of despair they raise questions about the meaning and purpose of life in general, and their life in particular. Some will withdraw from all familiar surroundings and entertain thoughts of suicide.

The resources of the Christian faith are helpful in assisting the parishioner in addressing the state of despair. One may argue that hope is the opposite of despair, and as Christians, we are always hoping that God will intervene in human affairs and improve the quality of our physical, emotional, psychological, and spiritual lives. We should also be hoping that God will bless (smile upon) and approve our thoughts and actions. It is human to despair. Mary and Martha were in a state of despair when Lazarus died (see John 11:1-43). Just as Jesus brought hope and healing to the lives of these two people in despair, the pastoral counselor has a responsibility to provide hope and healing to those parishioners who are in despair. Through the process of listening to the narrative of grief, and demonstrating and embodying empathy for the parishioner, the pastoral counselor may be able to help the parishioner cope with despair by placing it in a context. In other words, the parishioner should arrive at the conclusion that despair is a significant but temporal (passing) phase.

In some cases the normal and temporary despair of grief will deepen into a more serious and prolonged depression. The vigilant pastoral counselor will closely monitor any parishioner who seems stuck in the despair phase, and as needed, this person may be referred to a mental health professional who can better assess and treat clinical depression.

Reengagement in Life. Finally, a parishioner will emerge from the various stages of grief and choose to live life once again. This is not to say that all feelings of grief and loss are gone; most people will continue to feel occasional sadness, loneliness, and other emotions associated with loss. But the feelings will be more fleeting and often more seasonal or occasional, triggered by the time of year (e.g., anniversary, birthday, holiday), a location (e.g., site of death or of fond memories), or even a sensory experience (e.g., a particular scent, a beloved song, a particularly beautiful or poignant image). And while the parishioner may continue to receive support from family, friends, and institutions, he or she also begins to establish and achieve new and preexisting goals.

The pastoral counselor should recognize that the parishioner is coming to the end of the cycle of grief. During this final phase the pastoral counselor may assist in clarifying or establishing the parishioner's goals and encourage him or her to maintain the support and strategies previously developed to cope with resurgent feelings of anger or despair. Reassure the parishioner that you will continue to be a pastoral resource after the termination of formal counseling sessions.

Challenges in All Stages of Grief

The pastoral counselor may interact with people at all stages of the grief cycle. In their role as parish clergy, pastors may be present in the moment of death or in the hours and days that immediately follow as the news is processed and as decisions about the body, the funeral, and notifications of family and others must be made. In such instances the pastor is most likely to encounter the earlier stages of grief. In other instances survivors will reach out for pastoral support when the shock wears off, the funeral is over, and the reality of loss sets in. Then the pastoral counselor may face the middle stages of the grief process or perhaps a realization that the parishioner truly has not accepted the death as reality at all. And as suggested above, some people will seek counseling with various presenting problems, and only in the course of the intake interview will the pastoral counselor discover unresolved grief at the root.

Pastoral counseling sessions with individuals or families who have lost loved ones may resemble crisis counseling inasmuch as pastor and parishioner(s) may meet only on one occasion: an encounter that focuses on the planning of a funeral or memorial service. It is the pastor's responsibility to serve not only as official representative of the church but also as pastoral counselor who listens to the narrative and suggests ways in which the survivors can cope with their grieving.

Bereavement counseling is more complicated in a family setting, where each surviving individual may be processing the grief at a different pace or responding in different ways. Some may be in despair, and others caught in the heat of anger. Some may even be in denial, especially if they were not present in the moments and days following the death, or if they were unable to participate in the rituals of a funeral or memorial service. The pastoral counselor will need extra sensitivity in navigating the wide range of emotions and the reactions that grieving family members may have to one another. An important aspect of such counseling encounters is helping individual family members understand the stages of grief, the personal experiences of those stages, and the reality that there is no one "right" way to grieve.

Another challenge in bereavement counseling is the task of helping individuals move from one phase of grief to the next. Someone who assumes that sadness and despair are the language of grief may feel guilty or even unhinged when they experience the anger phase. The person who feels the despair fading may feel a measure of panic about moving into acceptance of the loss, perhaps fearing that acceptance means forgetting or forsaking the loved one.

Attend closely in the first counseling session with a bereaved individual or family. Listen to their tone of voice as well as their words. Are they coherent and rational, or are they rambling and mumbling? Notice their body language, from gestures and degree of eye contact to the angle of their body—toward the counselor as well as toward one another in a group setting. These observations will help the pastoral counselor to determine where each person is in the cycle of grief.

Recognize that the parishioner is telling the narrative of grief through a particular lens, be it one of denial, anger, or despair. The pastoral counselor should reflect empathy and compassion with both words and body language of his or her own. At all costs, do not attempt to rush a parishioner from one phase to the next. First, assist the survivor in discerning the phase of the grief cycle that he or she is currently in. Then, explain in simple and supportive words the nature of that particular phase and its relationship to the rest of the cycle.

Ultimately, pastoral counselors may want to offer assurance that they are available to journey with the parishioner throughout the process, and that there is indeed an end to the cycle—the proverbial light at the end of the tunnel. Indeed, there is truth in the metaphor of Scripture, "Weeping may linger for the night, but joy comes with the morning" (Psalm 30:5). This is not to say that the loss is ever erased. We are permanently affected by the change that comes with the death of a loved one, and that change goes deep when the loss is a traumatic one. However, the task of the pastoral counselor is to demonstrate how the resources of the Christian faith can assist the parishioner in leading a meaningful, productive, goal-oriented life beyond the intense and often wrenching initial process of grief.

38. The Role of Wounded Healer

As clergy as well as pastoral counselors, pastors regularly witness or preside over funerals at their churches. Generally, there is a degree of emotional distance between the pastor and the bereaved family; however, the clergy are intimately aware of the range of emotions being experienced by the family. In fact, I have seen services in which a person can hear the family crying while members of the clergy were sitting quietly but discreetly wiping tears from the eyes. In a true church family, when one grieves, in some way, we all grieve.

Some pastors may shed tears of empathy during their bereavement visits and grief counseling sessions, especially if the loss is a shared one. Such transparent empathy may enhance the therapeutic relationship between the pastoral counselor and counselee. It may assure the parishioner that the loss is real and grief is acceptable, that weeping is a healthy and normal expression of grief—it is okay to cry. Ultimately, such moments may assist the parishioner in processing and resolving his or her own cycle of grief.

There is a difference, however, between sharing in another's sorrow and projecting one's own unresolved grief on a bereaved parishioner. In one instance I was providing counseling to a family in which the husband, the father of two boys, had died just two weeks prior. The sons were eight and ten years old. As one of the boys began to talk about his beloved father, his voice cracked and his eyes began to well with tears. His story of a deep and permanent loss began to remind me of a significant loss that I had experienced in my life. I had to use every clinical technique and professional skill that I could think of to keep from weeping with the boy, as much for myself as for him.

In that moment I made a mental note of my feeling and managed to continue with the pastoral counseling session. Weeks after the session, and with the assistance of a pastoral counselor of my own, I began my own process of continuing to address a painful experience in my life so that I could be a more effective pastoral counselor in the future.

If the pastoral counselor has experienced the traumatic death of a friend, colleague, or family member, I strongly suggest resolving the issues regarding that grief prior to engaging in counseling with bereaved parishioners. Pastoral counseling sessions with parishioners are not an opportunity for the pastor to process unresolved personal grief. Nor are counseling sessions an opportunity to stifle the emotional responses of grieving parishioners because their story or tears will prompt the pastoral counselor to cry. Pastoral counselors must recognize that they are wounded healers who should demonstrate care for themselves as they demonstrate care for others. The Holy Spirit is indeed our Comforter. Pastoral counselors who have unresolved grief of their own should find time to commune and fellowship with the Holy Spirit. Professional pastoral counseling, in conjunction with God's abiding presence, will assist the counselor in resolving these issues.

Pastoral counseling is undoubtedly a stressful and arduous task. Relating to parishioners through their conflicts, anxieties and meandering personal narratives becomes all the more difficult when we are forced to draw from our well of theological and existential experiences that necessarily relate to the mental anguish, perceived spiritual alienation, and emotional suffering of others who find themselves enveloped in the cycle of grief. As pastors who recognize that the life and ministry of Jesus the Christ is our theological and practical point of departure, we readily embrace the idea that the Christian walk calls us to comfort others while they suffer, just as Christ comforts us while we suffer. Indeed, suffering is a universal experience; however, remember that we have an ever-present resource in the healing and life-sustaining power of God. The idea that God is comforter to both pastor and parishioner is captured by Paul in 2 Corinthians 1:3-4. He writes: "Praise be to the God and Father of our Lord Jesus Christ, the Father of compassion and the God of all comfort, who comforts us in all our troubles, so that we can comfort those in any trouble with the comfort we have received from God."

God's presence in the therapeutic moment is an unmistakable healing balm for counselor and counselee. It is an effective agent in the mental health and the holistic care of all of the members of the Christian community. As a pastoral counselor who ministers to others, however, be sure to secure care for yourself as a wounded healer. I encourage you to fully utilize the resources of God as revealed through the power and presence of the Holy Spirit. After all, pastoral counseling is distinct from other types of counseling in that the adjective *pastoral* necessarily precedes the term *counseling*; therefore, our overall effectiveness as pastoral counselors is inextricably connected to the pastoral or shepherding motif expressed through the values of the Good Shepherd (John 10:1-6). It is through our authentic and incessant love for God as well as our neighbor that we will be able to bring hope and healing to a suffering humanity through the pastoral counseling moment.

Initial Interview Form for the Pastoral Counselor

I. Background Information

_____
Name

_____
Address

_____
City, state, zip code

_____
Telephone number

_____
E-mail address

_____
Date of birth

_____
Emergency contact

II. Medical and Clinical Information

Are you currently under a doctor's care?   Yes _____ No _____

Are you currently taking medication for physical
or mental problems?   Yes _____ No _____

If yes, what medications are you taking? What is your diagnosis?

_____

_____

_____

Have you ever been hospitalized for physical, medical
or psychological reasons?   Yes _____ No _____

If yes, what were the dates of and reasons for your hospitalization?

_____

_____

_____

Do you have suicidal thoughts?   Yes _____ No _____

Do you have a plan to commit suicide?   Yes _____ No _____

Do you have a plan to hurt anyone
other than yourself?   Yes _____ No _____

III. Religious Information

Are you a Christian?   Yes _____ No _____

What is your denominational affiliation?

_____

Are you a member of this church?   Yes _____ No _____

If not, what is your church home?

_____

Are you formally requesting pastoral
counseling?   Yes _____ No _____

IV. In three sentences or less, please describe the nature of your problem.

_____

_____

_____

_____

_____

_____

_____

_____

Sample Code of Ministerial Ethics

The Covenant and Code of Ethics for Ministerial Leaders of American Baptist Churches

Having accepted God's call to leadership in Christ's Church, I covenant with God to serve Christ and the Church, and with the help of the Holy Spirit, to deepen my obedience to the Two Great Commandments: to love the Lord our God with all my heart, soul, mind, and strength, and to love my neighbor as myself.

In affirmation of this commitment, I will abide by the Code of Ethics of the Ministers Council of the American Baptist Churches and I will faithfully support its purposes and ideals. As further affirmation of my commitment, I covenant with my colleagues in ministry that we will hold one another accountable for fulfillment of all the public actions set forth in our Code of Ethics.

■ I will hold in trust the traditions and practices of our American Baptist Churches; I will not accept a position in the American Baptist family unless I am in accord with those traditions and practices; nor will I use my influence to alienate my congregation/constituents or any part thereof from its relationship and support of the denomination. If my convictions change, I will resign my position.

■ I will respect and recognize the variety of calls to ministry among my American Baptist colleagues and other Christians.

■ I will seek to support all colleagues in ministry by building constructive relationships wherever I serve, both with the staff where I work and with colleagues in neighboring churches.

■ I will advocate adequate compensation for my profession. I will help lay persons and colleagues to understand that ministerial leaders should not expect or require fees for pastoral services from constituents they serve when these constituents are helping pay their salaries.

■ I will not seek personal favors or discounts on the basis of my ministerial status.

■ I will maintain a disciplined ministry in such ways as keeping hours of prayers and devotion, endeavoring to maintain wholesome family relationships, sexual integrity, financial responsibility, and regularly engaging in educational and recreational activities for ministerial and personal development. I will seek to maintain good health habits.

■ I will recognize my primary obligation to the church or employing group to which I have been called, and will accept added responsibilities only if they do not interfere with the overall effectiveness of my ministry.

■ I will personally and publicly support my colleagues who experience discrimination on the basis of gender, race, ethnicity, age, marital status, national origin, physical impairment, or disability.

■ I will not proselytize from other Christian churches.

■ I will, upon my resignation or retirement, sever my ministerial leadership relations with my former constituents, and will not make ministerial contacts in the field of another ministerial leader without his/her request and/or consent.

■ I will hold in confidence and treat as confidential communication any information provided to me with the expectation of privacy. I will not disclose such information in private or public except when, in my practice of ministry, I am convinced that the sanctity of confidentiality is outweighed by my well-founded belief that life-threatening or substantial harm will be caused.

■ I will not use my ministerial status, position, or authority knowingly to abuse, misguide, negatively influence, manipulate, or take advantage of anyone, especially children.

■ I will report all instances of abuse as required by law to the appropriate agency. In any case involving persons working in ABC ministry, I will also report the circumstances to the appropriate regional and/or national denominational representative.

■ I will show my personal love for God as revealed in Jesus Christ in my life and ministry, as I strive together with my colleagues to preserve the dignity, maintain the discipline, and promote the integrity of the vocation to which we have been called.

_____

Signed

_____

Date

Reprinted from the website of the Ministers Council of the American Baptist Churches (www.ministerscouncil.com/WhoWeAre/documents/CodeofEthicsEng2010correction.pdf)

Designing a
Pastoral Counseling Program

A Vision from the Lord

There are numerous examples throughout the sixty-six books of the Bible that describe how a particular person's thoughts and actions were directly influenced by a vision or utterance from the Lord. The Old Testament prophets saw visions or heard a word from the Lord, and New Testament figures such as Jesus, Peter, and Paul had visions or heard a message from God. Proverbs 3:5-6 instructs us, "Trust in the LORD with all your heart, and do not rely on your own insight. In all your ways acknowledge him, and he will make straight your paths."

Has God placed it upon your heart as pastor or lay shepherd to begin a pastoral counseling ministry? Be sure that it is the Lord who is leading in that direction, since such a ministry involves a great deal of energy, resources, and passion, not only in the establishment and founding of the program but also in sustaining and growing the ministry.

How will the congregation perceive the idea of a counseling program? Be prepared to explore a variety of questions, including but not limited to these:

■ Will the counseling program be expected to provide a revenue stream (i.e., to generate income)? If so, decisions will need to be made related to a fee structure, salaries, licensing for the counselors, and administration of the financial and legal issues.

■ Will the church view the program as a means to provide more effective pastoral care only within the congregation or as a means of outreach to serve the community by welcoming external clientele? If the program is intended to serve both members and nonmembers, the church may need to consider marketing efforts to spread the word in the community.

■ What is the general attitude of church members toward mental health ministry? Some Christians, especially in certain cultures or traditions, associate a stigma with therapy of any kind. It may be viewed with suspicion as a secular science or with disdain, as if seeking counseling demonstrates a lack of faith.

■ Along similar lines, what will church members expect personally from pastoral counseling? Will they expect biblical principles to be combined with the best that psychotherapy and other mental health disciplines have to offer? Some education or reeducation of the congregation may be necessary as you move forward with plans for establishing the new ministry.

■ What outside resources will you need in order to develop and sustain a mental health ministry in the church? Advice from your insurance provider as well as from a local attorney who specializes in church or nonprofit organization is essential. Will you also need the support of other churches and faith communities to sustain the ministry, especially if it is designed as a revenue-generating and self-sustaining program?

■ Have you developed a survey or other assessment tool to determine the levels of interest and support among church members in founding a counseling program? If your own church members will not take advantage of the new ministry, then perhaps the time is not right to undertake such a program.

■ What type of counseling services will your program offer? Will the ministry provide only private sessions with individuals or couples and families, or will it also offer support groups facilitated by licensed professionals? Some ministries focus on more general areas such as family and marriage counseling. Others may develop specialties related to certain types of families (adoptive, blended, remarried, divorced) or to specific presenting problems (addiction, depression, abuse, grief). And some may prefer to feature counseling related to spiritual direction, vocational discernment, or life coaching.

These questions, among others, will be useful in clarifying the call you are hearing from God. The answers will assist you in refining the vision and tailoring your program to best meet the needs of your congregation and community.

Ultimately, the pastor or lay shepherd will need the help and power of the Holy Spirit to do God's work. The pastor must understand, enact, or embody the vision of God as its concerns his or her own congregation. If God's vision is not present, the work will be in vain.

Communicating the Vision

After the pastor is clear about the need to develop a pastoral counseling program, he or she needs to communicate that refined vision to a constituency within the church. The process of communicating the idea should conform to procedures already established in the church's by-laws or constitution for introducing a new ministry to the life of the church. Whether the initial proposal is made to the board of deacons, trustees, or elders, be intentional and clear about presenting both the ministry goals and the practical details for establishing the counseling program.

Do not be surprised if not everyone is immediately receptive to the new ministry, particularly in a congregation that is struggling financially, politically, or theologically. The pastor or lay shepherd might want to share the vision first with a few trusted leaders and solicit their honest feedback on the idea. Ideally, they will offer constructive criticism that will equip the pastor to fill in any gaps of information or explication. Be sure to welcome this feedback in the spirit that it is offered—toward a shared goal of clearly communicating the God-given vision for a ministry that has potential to transform lives and heal broken hearts.

Even after refining the proposal in response to this friendly feedback, the pastor should be ready to answer questions and address concerns from a larger board or committee. Resist the temptation to be defensive or dictatorial. The pastoral counseling program will be most effective and have the best chance of success if the leadership of the church is fully behind its ministry.

Presenting the Program

Take the time necessary to "package" the vision well. Explain it in theological, theoretical, and concrete terms. For example, the pastor may begin with a description of his or her own pastoral counseling experiences to date: "Over the past ten years I have provided pastoral counseling to hundreds of church members. Most of those individuals, couples, and families have later shared how tremendously blessed they were by this ministry. Many have also asked if counseling services could be expanded to help additional people in the church and in the wider community."

Next, the pastor will want to talk about the leading that he or she has felt from God and a basic overview of the envisioned program itself. For example, "Over the years I have reflected deeply about those comments, and the Lord has placed it upon my heart to develop a formal pastoral counseling ministry in our church. I believe that God is leading us to design a ministry to provide pastoral counseling to individuals, couples, and families who are experiencing problems in three key areas: grief, substance abuse, and unemployment. It will be a ministry designed to convey the love of God and assist people in resolving real conflicts and problems in their inner and external relationships."

Now is the opportunity to talk more pragmatically about the specific model and how it will be crafted. Demonstrate the research and planning already invested in clarifying the vision, as well as details related to staffing, facilities, and timeline. For example, "Our pastoral counseling program will be modeled after the successful programs offered by Mount Gilead Baptist Church, Agape Congregational Church, and St. Andrew's Roman Catholic Church. The program will be staffed by three licensed and ordained members of our ministry team, who will receive additional clinical training from the local university. The program is tentatively scheduled to launch two years from now, after we have prepared office space to house the confidential counseling sessions and the administrative functions of the program."

Finally, invite questions from the board or committee that makes up your audience. This is an initial question-and-answer session to address big-picture concerns about the model: the target population and statistics related to their current emotional, psychological, and economic needs; the facilities and staffing needed; the confidential nature of the counseling process itself; any support or networking needed or already secured from other persons or institutions; the ministry goals and how they will be measured; and so on. At this stage, avoid getting entangled matters of numbers and fine print by deflecting questions about specific details (fees, insurance, overhead, etc.) until after the second half of your presentation—the business model.

Developing a Preliminary Business Model A certain constituency within every church is concerned (and perhaps even obsessed) with the idea of cost. Before the pastor can even form the words to say, "I have a great idea," these members will quickly respond, "But how much will it cost?" Given today's economic climate and the state of most churches' endowments, their point is well-taken. Even the pastor with a profound faith in God's provision has a responsibility to present the officers of the church with a model for sustaining and growing a new ministry.

I use the term *business model* as opposed to *business plan* at this phase in the process because in most cases a model is sufficient for the initial presentation to the leaders of the church. However, assuming that those leaders come on board with the vision, the pastor will go on to develop a detailed business plan in conjunction with the church officers. Such a plan should identify alternate revenue streams for the ministry in light of an ever-changing economic landscape.

To clarify the distinction between a business model and a business plan, a business model identifies a realistic budget with projected revenue, expenses, and a list of several potential funding streams (written into the church budget; third-party billing through insurance companies; fees paid by the clientele; support of a grant or foundation). A business plan adds more specifics, such as which streams will be tapped and the dollar amounts allocated from each stream, in addition to including elements such as an executive summary, company overview, business environment, company description, company strategy, marketing plan, and action plan.[1]

The business model and business plan are designed primarily to describe the ways in which the leaders of the local church plan to identify, amass, and distribute funds in order to build a pastoral counseling program. The thrust of the business plan and model is financial or economic in nature, and neither the plan nor the model is capable of providing the leadership of the church with a concise strategy or blueprint for assessing and implementing the entire pastoral counseling program.

In order to successfully implement this pastoral counseling program, the leadership of the church will need a blueprint called a "strategic plan" in order to implement both the business model and the business plan. A strategic plan will identify objectives, team members, strategies, and evaluation measures. A strategic plan provides the church leaders and congregation with a comprehensive but concise picture of how to develop and implement the pastoral counseling program; however, this strategy is not limited to money or the economic considerations of a business model or a business plan.

The strategic plan identifies and evaluates all aspects of the pastoral counseling program. For example, in the section titled "evaluation measures" the strategic plan can even evaluate the success of the business plan and quickly tell the leadership of the church if the business plan (e.g., how much money was raised and spent in relation to the number of people who were counseled as well as the quality of the counseling) was effective or ineffective. This concise document should be revised on an annual basis in light of the data (e.g., the results of the congregational survey and a survey given to the people who received pastoral counseling) that the church leadership receives regarding the pastoral counseling program. (For an example of a strategic plan that can be implemented in the local church, see appendix D.)

Some churches will attempt to formally launch a pastoral counseling ministry without adequate internal or external funding. Their rationale is rooted in an attempt to meet the needs of a suffering constituency while believing that God will make economic provisions for them. How much better it would be to practice wise stewardship and trust in God by saying, "We affirm the call and vision to found a pastoral counseling ministry at our church. It is not in the budget for this year, however. When we identify and obtain the appropriate financial resources, we will begin to implement the vision that God has for our church." Why better? Because if the program fails because of inadequate funding, it will be all the more difficult to gain support for the vision in the future.

It may be that certain aspects of a more comprehensive pastoral counseling program can and should move forward in the meantime. For example, the pastor may discern willing volunteers with expertise and energy to form support groups that require minimal funding to support. Or the ministerial staff may choose to begin training at the local seminary or university to prepare themselves for new responsibilities to come.

The pastor must be in constant communion with God and with the leadership of the church regarding the ideal time to launch the ministry. Pastoral leadership demands interplay between the spiritual and the pragmatic. It is through this creative tension that a new ministry will come into existence and find expression within the hearts and minds of a local Christian community.

Revenue Streams for the Program
Fee Schedule. Some pastoral counseling ministries charge a fee for their services. In many cases the fee schedule is based on a sliding scale. In other words,

because the services are first and foremost a ministry, the fees are adjusted based on the household income of the individual, couple, or family. Generally, that sliding fee scale ranges from $20 to $100 per hour. I recommend collecting the fee prior to the counseling session. Such a sliding-fee scale may be implemented in combination with other revenue streams.

Underwriting with Tithes and Offerings. Since members already give to the church in tithes and offerings, they may resist the idea of paying additional monies in order to receive pastoral counseling. After all, pastoral salaries are usually funded through the contributions of church members. So, if the church leadership is reluctant to charge parishioners a fee, the pastoral counseling program may be incorporated into the church's annual budget. A line item can be created in the annual budget called "pastoral counseling ministry." For each minister designated to perform pastoral counseling, consider allotting $5,200 annually (or approximately $100 per week) to perform five hours of pastoral counseling per week. Because the entire church body may need to vote on this financial addition to the budget, it is essential that the pastor has secured support for the counseling ministry from the leadership prior to bringing it before the church body.

Another possibility is for the church to underwrite counseling services for members in good standing and to establish a fee scale for external clients.

Third-party Billing. Parishioners seeking pastoral counseling necessarily want their pastor to embrace a particular theological perspective. The very discussions of Christian ethics, themes, figures, and norms that parishioners value within the pastoral counseling session may prohibit the church from receiving funding from the government, insurance agencies, or philanthropists. If the church wants its members to receive counseling but has no money to underwrite a pastoral counseling program, its leaders may have to create a separate nonprofit corporation (with 501c3 status) in order to receive support from the aforementioned agencies. The counseling that is received may not be explicitly Christian or "pastoral" in nature; however, the creation of this nonprofit would ensure that parishioners received mental health services from competent and licensed mental health professionals.

In short, the pastor and leadership team of the local church must take into consideration a number of factors (e.g., financial, spiritual, and political) prior to launching a successful pastoral counseling program. The leadership team may determine by using surveys, focus groups, or other qualitative and quantitative measures that there is a need for a comprehensive pastoral counseling program. God is sure to supply the vision as to how to implement it. Parishioners will always have problems that need to be discussed in an individual or group setting; therefore, the designers of the pastoral counseling ministry must embrace the idea that they have made a commitment to a long-term as opposed to a short-term ministry. My observations of local churches for the past thirty years indicate that many ministries are begun but often lose momentum over time (e.g., an exercise ministry or the floral ministry). The pastoral counseling ministry, because of its significance in the lives of individuals, couples, and families, cannot be list among these "ministry casualties." With careful planning, an authentic vision from God, and a dedicated team of professionals within and outside of the church, the pastoral counseling ministry is destined to be a success in the local church.

Notes

1. Steven D. Peterson, Peter E. Jaret, and Barbara Findlay Schenck, *Business Plan Kits for Dummies* (Hoboken, NJ: Wiley Publishing, 2005), 15–16.

SAMPLE STRATEGIC PLAN

Preliminary Steps for Developing a Pastoral Counseling Ministry

OBJECTIVES	TEAM MEMBERS	STRATEGIES	EVALUATION MEASURES
1.1 Assess the need for pastoral counseling in the church.	Pastor, governing board, someone to conduct field research and analysis of the data.	■ Design a congregational survey to assess the level of interest in a pastoral counseling program. ■ Ask church members to complete the anonymous survey following service.	■ Determine the response rate (i.e., percentage of congregants who completed the survey). ■ Analyze the data of the survey. Determine the level of interest. If so, in what areas?
1.2 Assess the current resources of the church.	Pastoral ministry team.	■ Determine who is qualified to provide pastoral counseling in the church (e.g. who is licensed/ordained; who has experience in pastoral counseling). ■ Encourage ministerial staff to take one or more courses in pastoral counseling at an accredited seminary. (First assess the quality of those courses.)	■ Count the number of people who are able to provide pastoral counseling. ■ Build the program around these current resources of the church and add to these resources.
1.3 Share the strategic plan with members of the governing boards of the church.	Pastor and people who are employed in human-service industries.	■ Create a PowerPoint presentation to share the need for a pastoral counseling program with the leadership of the church.	■ Substantiate your claims about the people's needs with data provided by credible websites (e.g., government website).

OBJECTIVES	TEAM MEMBERS	STRATEGIES	EVALUATION MEASURES
		■ Host a workshop within the church in order to teach congregants about the need for pastoral counseling.	■ Pay particular attention to statistics that focus on poverty, divorce, children, and drug addiction.
1.4 Research successful pastoral counseling programs in churches throughout the United States.	Pastoral ministry team, members of agencies such as the American Association of Pastoral Counselors (AAPC), churches that have successful counseling programs.	■ Visit churches with successful pastoral counseling ministries. ■ Solicit advice from the local representatives of agencies such as the American Association of Pastoral Counselors (AAPC). ■ Make a list of the resources (e.g. human, capital, and financial) that are needed to launch the ministry.	■ Include a minimum of twenty churches in this study. ■ Quantify their resources. Determine the extent to which your church's resources reflect their recourses. ■ Establish a timeline. ■ Meet with several agencies and individuals who are currently performing pastoral counseling.
1.5 Provide pastoral counseling to individuals, couples, and families	Pastoral ministry team, church leaders.	■ Market this new ministry to the church members through the bulletin and website.	■ Record the number of individuals, couples, and families who have requested or received pastoral counseling. ■ Use this number as your baseline. Add to this number in subsequent years.

GOAL: To create a pastoral counseling ministry in the local church in order to address the spiritual needs of individuals, couples, and families.